MW00780355

LEGAL FICTIONS

LEGAL

Fictions

CONSTITUTING

RACE,

COMPOSING

LITERATURE

KARLA FC HOLLOWAY

DUKE UNIVERSITY PRESS   DURHAM AND LONDON   2014

© 2014 Duke University Press
All rights reserved
Printed in the United States of
America on acid-free paper ∞
Designed by Amy Ruth Buchanan
Typeset in Arno Pro by Tseng
Information Systems, Inc.

Library of Congress
Cataloging-in-Publication Data
Holloway, Karla F. C., 1949–
Legal fictions : constituting race, composing
literature / Karla FC Holloway.
p. cm.
Includes bibliographical references and index.
ISBN 978-0-8223-5581-6 (cloth : alk. paper)
ISBN 978-0-8223-5595-3 (pbk. : alk. paper)
1. American literature — African American
authors — History and criticism. 2. African
Americans — Legal status, laws, etc. — History.
3. Race discrimination — Law and legislation —
United States — History. 4. Race in literature.
I. Title.
PS153.N5H64 2014
305.896′073 — dc23
2013025467

For Russell . . .
It's the last leaf.

....

CONTENTS

....

"Consult the text!"

—Ralph Ellison

A substantial history documents a persistent anxiety of influence in African American letters. Ralph Ellison's terse response about his own literary influences reflects this anxiety, as he made clear that a careful reading of his work, rather than any presumptive relationship to other writers (specifically other black writers), would sufficiently attest to his intellectual biography. When Ellison did acknowledge Richard Wright as his literary progenitor he qualified the relationship: "I respected Wright's work and I knew him, but this is not to say that he 'influenced' me as significantly as you assume. Consult the text! I sought out Wright because I had read Eliot, Pound, Gertrude Stein and Hemingway. . . . And Malraux and Dostoievsky and Faulkner, were 'ancestors'—if you please or don't please!"[1]

Despite his wistful originalism, Ellison does claim some literary kinfolk even though the weight of authors listed makes it evident that his effort was to broaden his literary progenitors rather than to limit it to what was, during his era, a reasonable association of other writers who were black, like him.

One might consider this focus on literary kinship a consequence of a well-developed argument regarding African American letters that sought a history, evidence that it did not, like Tospy, "jes grew." Specialists in the discipline went to great lengths to consider the socialities implicit in the racial subjects of African American literature. These histories led to a long century of searching for critically distinct tropes of black literature that would not only legitimate its presence but also give critical evidence of an evolutionary formulation. One might argue that African America's literary history paralleled African Americans' own history of personhood, in which the first task was to prove we were fully human rather than the fractional persons the Constitution declared us to be. For a good part of the twentieth century the effort to recover the cultural engagements of this literary history was found a continent away. Whether it was the oft-remarked-on trope of call and response, or a search for other dimensions of African ancestry and influences, the appeal of West Africa was rich with potential.[2] In retrospect, and despite the reach across the middle passage that theorists engaged in, the origins of U.S. black literatures seems closer to home and critically related to the processes and patterns of proof the nation ordinarily recognized. Black folks and black literature were equally bound, and determined, by law.

When enslaved Africans in America wrote autobiography and memoir and claimed their membership in a human race with narratives that opened with some version of "I was born," it was a form of black back talk to the Constitution of the newly formed nation. Article 1, Section 2, of The Constitution of the United States of America—the three-fifths clause, also known as the representation clause—relegated blacks to a fractional humanity. But the voices and bodies of the enslaved, a bitterly fought war, and the deeply embedded political and economic presence of Africans in America led to the document's eventual amendment. The civil rights amendments of the 1860s, specifically the Fourteenth Amendment's grant of the right to citizenship, were the constitutional response to the claim of natural origin and full personhood. But the evolution of legal text did not, however, fully and/or finally determine social act.

Over the course of a century and a half since the amended constitution gave blacks full citizenship, vicious patterns of denial, disparagement, and

Figure 1. President Lyndon Johnson signs the 1964 Civil Rights Bill. Reverend Martin Luther King Jr. stands behind the president, amongst the official overseers. LBJ Library photo by Cecil Stoughton.

unequal treatment led civil rights activists and demonstrators — especially during the 1960s — to repeat a twentieth-century version of their forbearers' claims. These activists marched through the streets of the United States with visible singularity. A textual consistency and a legal history emerged from their social activism. After generations of struggle, a perverse and finely practiced craft in black deaths and dismemberments, fire hosings and beatings by civilian law enforcers, the Civil Rights Act of 1964 was passed as a legislative response to the disorder of the era. Activist preacher Martin Luther King Jr. stood over President Lyndon Johnson's shoulder as he signed the bill into law.

Despite the landmark status of this legislation's resolution to civil disenfranchisement, and despite the intervening years since its passage, the sociality implicit in the claim to rights was unfulfilled. And the text that best represented the justice denied was not explicitly legal. Instead,

Figure 2. "I *AM* A MAN"; photograph of Memphis Sanitation Workers Strike. March 28, 1968. Courtesy of photographer Richard L. Copley. Copyright Richard L. Copley.

the evidence of its focus was substantive personhood. This claim to the rights of man was accorded to persons whose national citizenship became legally cognizable. But their social personhood was still contested. The sociality of the claim proved to be the more difficult boundary. The plain statement reflecting the lacunae was printed on placards and banners and was stark in its simplicity. It was a nouveau version of the argument their eighteenth- and nineteenth-century ancestors had to make regarding their own rights to full legal personhood: "I *AM* A MAN."

The 1964 legislation crafted a recognizable architecture for the movement of marches and demonstrations. In an appreciable irony, Reverend Martin Luther King Jr., who stood among the distinguished array of gentlemen (only) in the elegant and pristine environs of the White House ceremony, was the man to lead the 1968 strike by sanitation workers who marched through malodorous and garbage-laden Memphis streets carrying aloft the "I *Am* A Man" placards.

Despite the scores of years of marching, declarations, protests, and street rebellions, the twentieth century's legal reasoning regarding black identity did not end with the turn of the century or the implementation of strong and declarative civil rights legislation. Early in the twenty-first century, another version of the dispute regarding a black person's claim to legal personhood emerged. This time it was not a race, but a representative of the race in the spectacular body of a president whose claim to his office was disputed by some, on the spurious basis of his official personhood residing outside of the laws that would otherwise permit his occupancy of the office of the president. Certainly there were some in the nation who could not abide the thought that a black commander-in-chief and his family were the official residents of the White House. But the spoken challenge to Barack Obama's legitimate occupancy of the office of the president (notably, a property as well as a citizenship claim) rendered to some this presidency as illegal, invisible, and quite literally without standing in regard to his claim to the nation's highest elected office. Indeed, the notion of criminal trespass was as relevant as other notions refocused on the meaning of the constitution's language of "natural-born," a verbiage with a particularly vexed history when it came to persons whose bodies were once constitutionally declared to be only partial persons. With a respectful nod to Aretha Franklin, we might reasonably recall her 1967 single and ask what does it take to "feel like a natural (wo)man?"

Despite the legal document that the president's office proffered as evidence of his rightful claim to a federally viable citizenship—specifically a birth certificate from the State of Hawaii indicating that he was indeed born in the United States—the expediency of "birtherism" claimed for itself more viability than the legal document.[3] Indeed, it paralleled the way in which legislation attached to the claim of black bodies found the sociality of race a persistently substantive and even dependable site of discord.

This most recent claim of legal personhood is different in text but not very different in substance from the "I was born" declaration of enslaved and formerly enslaved Africans in the eighteenth and nineteenth centuries. And it seems eminently reasonable to recognize its relatedness to

STATE OF HAWAII   CERTIFICATE OF LIVE BIRTH   DEPARTMENT OF HEALTH

FILE NUMBER **151**   **61 10641**

1a. Child's First Name (Type or print)	1b. Middle Name	1c. Last Name
BARACK	HUSSEIN	OBAMA, II

2. Sex	3. This Birth	4. If Twin or Triplet, Was Child Born	5a. Birth Date	Month	Day	Year	5b. Hour
Male	Single ☒ Twin ☐ Triplet ☐	1st ☐ 2nd ☐ 3rd ☐		August	4,	1961	7:24 P.M.

6a. Place of Birth: City, Town or Rural Location: Honolulu   6b. Island: Oahu

6c. Name of Hospital or Institution (If not in hospital or institution, give street address): Kapiolani Maternity & Gynecological Hospital

6d. Is Place of Birth Inside City or Town Limits? If no, give judicial district: Yes ☒ No ☐

7a. Usual Residence of Mother: City, Town or Rural Location: Honolulu   7b. Island: Oahu   7c. County and State or Foreign Country: Honolulu, Hawaii

7d. Street Address: 6085 Kalanianaole Highway

7e. Is Residence Inside City or Town Limits? If no, give judicial district: Yes ☒ No ☐

7f. Mother's Mailing Address:

7g. Is Residence on a Farm or Plantation? Yes ☐ No ☒

8. Full Name of Father	9. Race of Father
BARACK HUSSEIN OBAMA	African

10. Age of Father	11. Birthplace (Island, State or Foreign Country)	12a. Usual Occupation	12b. Kind of Business or Industry
25	Kenya, East Africa	Student	University

13. Full Maiden Name of Mother	14. Race of Mother
STANLEY ANN DUNHAM	Caucasian

15. Age of Mother	16. Birthplace (Island, State or Foreign Country)	17a. Type of Occupation Outside Home During Pregnancy	17b. Date Last Worked
18	Wichita, Kansas	None	

18. I certify that the above stated information is true and correct to the best of my knowledge. [signature] Ann Dunham Obama

18a. Signature of Parent or Other Informant — Parent ☒ Other ☐

18b. Date of Signature: 8-7-61

19. I hereby certify that this child was born alive on the date and hour stated above. [signature] David A. Sinclair

19a. Signature of Attendant — M.D. ☒ D.O. ☐ Midwife ☐ Other ☐

19b. Date of Signature: 8.8.61

20. Date Accepted by Local Reg. AUG -8 1961

21. Signature of Local Registrar [signature] U K Lee

22. Date Accepted by Reg. General AUG -8 1961

23. Evidence for Delayed Filing or Alteration

APR 25 2011

I CERTIFY THIS IS A TRUE COPY OR ABSTRACT OF THE RECORD ON FILE IN THE HAWAII STATE DEPARTMENT OF HEALTH

Alvin T. Onaka, Ph.D.
STATE REGISTRAR

Figure 3. President Barack Obama's official long-form birth certificate.

the text on the placards of 1960s era civil rights demonstrators. From the perspective of these interlocking histories, the perplexing foolishness that led the forty-fourth president of the United States to have to produce some legal document that had federal standing to prove his own statutory claim finds its location in a story of origins that arguably makes some sense out of the nonsense of the "birthers'" arguments about the legitimacy of his citizenship. It is all, finally, an origin story that finds its genesis and arguably its resolution in the law.

The link of events from the eras of enslavement, civil rights activism, and the politics of a black presidency illustrates how issues of personhood and race in America were persistently seen as legal questions that revealed a nearly intractable sociality. In other words, U.S. racialisms were attached to America's legal and social histories in ways that argued both for their disciplinary distinctiveness as well as their insistent association. Although there is ample evidence for the legal history, it is also the case that African American fiction's literary imagination folded these claims into a tradition that still holds onto a constructedness of race that depends as much on the social as it is constituted and finds its resolutions in narratives that are, like their histories, bound by law.

Bound by Law

The racial politics that enveloped the presidency of Barack Hussein Obama are a fitting touchstone for the issues I focus on in this book. Although plenty of folks anticipated that the first black president would put to rest or at least settle or even reasonably calm some of the historic racial tensions in American society, the perversity was that Barack Obama's presidency carved out a new space for extraordinary racial vitriol, racial obsessiveness, and racial panic. Instead of a postracial society in which this difference matters less, race, the infamous Du Boisian color line, entrenched separatisms located in matters of embodied differences, identity politics, and identity policies became at least as serious a facet of twenty-first century life as they had been in the life of the nineteenth and twentieth centuries. These issues have instantiated a difference of substance, but not of kind. Our shadows linger and leak. They seep from mottled grey and scaffold scalar recollections. They assure our potential, securing it by ways and means at once penumbral and exquisite. They instantiate things remembered past their time, promised beyond situation. Race still matters in twenty-first-century America in ways that reinforce two centuries of institutionalized harms.

Perhaps there was reason to suspect that this would be the pattern. Our legislative responses to differences that provoke social bias encourage the country to notice difference in order to discount it. Consequently we have developed into a nation that is both practiced in and intensely dedicated to using race as a metric for voting patterns, education policies and outcomes, medical assessments, predictors of social and economic success, housing choices, incarceration patterns, aspirational objectives, religion, and just about every means of stratification in both our public and private lives in order to better understand what U.S. socialities mean. In order to accomplish that objective, we deploy the filter of "race" even though the meaning of the word is as vague, haphazard, illogical, variable, and happenstance today as it was in the first years of the nation's founding. In fact, our preoccupation with discerning race—regardless of good or ill intent—has contributed to its perception as a category of difference that has discernible rigor. The (suspect) ability to distinguish race arguably renders the assignation appropriate and the enterprise reasonable. Our national habit of performing and validating racial assignments as if they are coherent and correct persists even though our experiences with race indicate its categorical incoherence (is Barack Obama a black president or another white one?), and twenty-first century genomic science reveals there is no molecular component of biological life that matches social perceptions of racial difference. In fact, the mapping of the human genome revealed the fiction of race as an insular and identifiable biological category. Humans are distinct from nonhumans but not from other human beings. Despite this scientific understanding, in a country that arguably values science and celebrates reason, it has done little to lead us away from reifying racial difference as normative and discoverable. In fact, even scientific research ignores its own findings as it racially aggregates populations for clinical research, sometimes directly under the authorization of governmental regulatory agencies.[1] As a result and despite its origin as a convenient fiction of political design and economic expediency, America's invention of race as a way of assigning legal and social rights and determining political legitimacy is (perhaps) its most visible, predictable, persistent, and paradoxical social convention.

Even during the many years when this nation focused on a body of laws—immigration policies that codified the Constitution's language of "natural born citizen" (Art. 2, Sect. 1) — it did not experience the degree of intensity and breadth of scrutiny that the body of the nation's first black president provoked. In an effort to delegitimize his occupancy of the office, his father's birthplace (Kenya) and the fabrication that President Obama was not born in the United States brought this language of "natural born citizen" into critical interrogation. Each of the words in that phrase has become a contemporary site of contestation that rehearses centuries of legal personhood that designates who might be entitled to constitutionally derived rights. What does it mean to be "natural"? Does it modify "born," or is it a particular kind of nominative? And how might a "citizen" be qualified?

Buried within the logical pretense of these interpretive queries is the undead interrogative that has historically attached itself to U.S. black bodies — the question that prompted David Walker's famous 1830 appeal "Are we men?–I ask you Oh my brethren, are we Men?"; Sojourner Truth's 1851 plea "Ain't I a Woman?"; and the 1968 protest's declarative reprise "I *Am* A Man!"[2] The politics embedded in this pattern of repetition anticipates the interrogative that called for the president of the United States to release evidentiary proof, which effectively legalizes the inquiry. It is an act that repeats the ways in which legally inscrutable bodies act up, resist regulation, strike, and protest. And one of them, in an ultimate act of insistent visibility, has even disrupted the visibly coherent line of U.S. presidents. There is an out(side of)law and irregular quality to embodied blackness. And for this book, as well as in the general body of work, this is familiar terrain.

As an academic writer, issues of text and body have interested me in nearly every exploration, critique, theorization, or casual consideration of the construction of narrative. I reflected on the intersections of text and embodiment most recently in *Private Bodies, Public Texts* (2011) and explored the habits of my own writing and reading and the history of black books in *BookMarks: Reading in Black and White* (2006). In its way, this manuscript is a theoretical postscript to *BookMarks* as it interrogates the twinned literary embodiment and constitutional origins of racialized notice—what makes a body visible enough for literary act and legal notice?

Legal Fictions considers the origin and the persistence of the constitutive legal boundedness of black identity in the United States. It interrogates the ways in which the substantive presence of a legally inscribed and constituted body adheres to this nation's literary fiction as well as to the facts of the nation's social, cultural, and political evolution. The association between law and personhood is especially vigorous in United States black (or "African-American") literature. In my judgment, this relational association has extended itself to the ways in which we constitute national identity and character (even when they are fictions); the ways in which we imagine and structure narrative; and the ways in which our stories reflect U.S. cultures.

The association of my legal interest to the literary has its origin in the supple and provocative argument that Toni Morrison advances in *Playing in the Dark: Whiteness and the Literary Imagination.*[3] In fact, it is Morrison's particular perspective in that text that an "Africanist" presence in the United States is consequentialist and has left its imaginative toll—indeed a visible mark—in the fictions of U.S. literatures that leads me to consider the legal construction of that literary imagination. If Morrison's argument is correct that a haunting black presence permeates American literature, what, then, is its formulation in black American literatures? *Playing in the Dark*'s focus on white writers' fictions engages the ways in which their imaginations are (arguably legally) entailed by their inability to escape the race or their inability to "play" *outside* of the dark. It's helpful to notice that Morrison's idea of play comes with a particular kind of rule boundedness that is like law. It appears as if she is both implicitly and explicitly interested in the rules of the game. In her preface Morrison asks these questions: "How is 'literary whiteness' and 'literary blackness' made, and what is the consequence of that construction? How do embedded assumptions of racial (not racist) language work in the literary enterprise?" (1993, xii).

This book takes the structural and cognizable association of law and literature as its text. I read Morrison's interest as an inquiry into a persistently regulatory authority that is (perhaps perversely) dependent on a presumptive binary of literary lawlessness, a fugitivity that black texts "play" against. The answer to "how is literary blackness made?" is both structural and spatial. It is, in fact, most evident in narratives that explore what happens when rules are contested, absent, or irregular. And these considerations are often the contextual evidence of the *outlaw* consequence—the *fugitivity* in the dark.[4]

Intimate Intersectionalities — Scalar Recollections

The plain statement that frames this manuscript is that U.S. racial identity is a constructed legal fiction. Although the origins of racial differentiation lie within the law, racial identitarianism has an absolutely persistent political and social iteration that gains a substantive and familiar presence through its consistent and evolving engagements even, and especially, when these are a fiction. However, rather than achieving some cognizable or visible coherence from a familiar black literary subjectivity, the evolving matter of identity comes to reflect the kind of destabilization that is notable in poststructuralist theory as it becomes merely an evidentiary fragment in what is best understood as a vast postmodernist collage.

There is a mind-boggling array of twentieth- and twenty-first-century variations of literary blackness that incorporates the essence of Ralph Ellison's most widely read novel, *Invisible Man*. Ellison's eponymous character is disabled by his visible incoherence, especially in the way that it is tied to his ability to inflict anarchy on a growing company of folk who encounter him.[5] An arguably perverse version of liberation consistently challenges the changing forms of his evolving (postmodernist) subject and subsequently gives him at least a pseudo, if not a utilitarian, coherence binding the locative parallelism between coexisting states of freedom and enslavement. In this long evolution, freedom and enslavement become at least prosaically equivalent to states of being—locations as geographically viable as that which the enslaved might occupy (or flee from). In fact, whether and to the extent that one is enslaved or free displaces other reasonable forms of identity and becomes the substance of race matters.

In the socialities represented in U.S. fiction, a subjective ontology is accomplished through the associative link between being and location. The aspirational site marked by the North Star becomes a destination as much as it situates the *idea* of freedom. But a subject's legal boundedness is tied not simply to (for example) whether or not he makes it to Canada, but the persistence and factual reality and reach of racial jurisprudence — slave catchers for whom no state or country boundary was an obstacle. Laws that enumerated, codified, structured, and regulated an enslaved person's body assured racial identity's viable and arguably coercive presence. Whether law was used to designate a slave or to free her, the contingent relationship between laws that regulated the bodies and (states of) being became the legacy of U.S. black identity.

Law and literature both depend on a critical intimacy with the ways and means of language. Like legal precedent, literature retains its connection to some notion of a scripted past through allusion. An argument that claims racial legibility as a sustained legal fiction depends on an evident trace of that past, a noticeable architecture by which race and law might leak into our fictions.

As visibly substantive a history as the past provides for law and literature, history is ultimately effaced by the heft of judicial formations and literary structures that render the actual past less necessary than the fictions that come to represent it. Morrison calls these "rememories" in her novel *Beloved*, an illustration that I will turn to shortly. However, when what emerges from the past is ontological, the visible embodiment of a racial legibility that matters renders the stakes substantially higher.

In law, this social narrative found its own peculiar composition. Consider the legal documentation of a harm done to Lydia, an enslaved woman of African descent and the property of Elizabeth Jones. Jones resided in Chowan County, North Carolina, and had occasion to hire Lydia out to John Mann. At the district court level, Mann was charged with criminal assault for shooting her during an event that happened during his lease. Mann was rendered up before a jury for trial. The trial court determined that Mann's shooting was disproportionately punitive and fined him five dollars. Mann appealed the ruling to the state Supreme Court.[6]

The 1829 North Carolina State Supreme Court ruling explains the parameters of the case—that "battery was committed during the period of hiring"—and clarifies the "enquiry" as to "whether a cruel and unreasonable battery on a slave, by the hirer, is justifiable" (*State v. Mann* 1829, 265). Notably Judge Ruffin's decision was not based on whom Lydia belonged to at the time—whether it was rightly Elizabeth Jones or Mann; rather he affirmatively declares that "our laws uniformly treat the master or other person having the possession and command of the slave, as entitled to the same extent of authority. . . . The object is the same." It is "the services of the slave." And if further clarification and moral distancing is appropriate, he offers these as well in this section of his judgment: "The power of the master must be absolute, to render the submission of the slave perfect. I most freely confess my sense of the harshness of this proposition; I feel it as deeply as any man can. . . . But in the actual condition of things, it must be so. There is no remedy. *This discipline belongs to the state of slavery*" (ibid., 266, 267, my emphasis).

The decision rendered in *State v. Mann* turned on the very issue that is at the core of this book. The legal arguments folded into a property claim reaches into issues of contract, evidence, and rights. It absolutely mirrors the appellate argument advanced by Mann. And it has a history in continental law that is necessary to remember. Sovereign power meant authority over life and death. Consider this Roman history when we think of contemporary debates regarding abortion legislation and the way in which they echo a version of *patria* (father) to dispose of a child's life as well as a slave's. Knowing the history of *patria potestas* (power of a father) might reasonably lead one to argue that the abortion debate is actually a debate about who should have this authority rather than the nature of the authority. When Mann argued that his assault or battery on his slave was fully within his rights, he based his claim not only on a cultural notion of sovereignty, but on its related legal claim as a property owner. At the state supreme court, Judge Thomas Ruffin agreed with his defense, noting that "the power of the master must be absolute, to render the slave perfect" (ibid., 266). In his judgment, slavery mandated an "uncontrolled authority over the body" and the slave was "doomed in his own person, and his posterity, to live without . . . the capacity to make anything his own" (ibid., 266). *State v. Mann* contains critical language that underscores the constitutional conviction that separated bodies of slaves from the personage of citizens.[7]

In *The History of Sexuality*, Foucault understands this evolving but omnipresent principle in his discussion of sovereignty. "At stake is the biological existence of a population" he writes. But Foucault also determines that biology is "no longer the juridical existence of sovereignty."[8] I would argue the point still obtains, albeit with a slight but critical distinction. The juridical is both exposed and essential. And sovereignty has become the sine qua non of constitutionalism. The site of interpretive power lies with the constitutional authority invested in and constitutive of the Supreme Court. It operates as the embodiment of sovereign state doctrine. Centuries of American biosocialities have mirrored that conviction, often formulated from the very complexity of embodied identity—who might be (or become) a legal person and therefore worthy of the rights of man.

From this perspective and as bodies of law, matters of captivity and freedom are fecund literary sites. Their notable literatures, including Harriet Beecher Stowe's *Uncle Tom's Cabin* (1852)—a novel that references the Mann case—include a wealth of narratives and fictions written by enslaved or formerly enslaved persons. It is perfectly reasonable to expect these historically imagined narratives to proliferate during the era of U.S. slavery. But why would a particular literary discipline repeat these forms well past the era of legalized slavery and with such regularity? Long past the eighteenth and nineteenth centuries, when, given the entrenched patterns and social consequences of enslavement, one might reasonably predict the genre's emergence and popularity, we find its odd persistence in the libraries of mid-twentieth and these first decades of the twenty-first century, where works like Margaret Walker's *Jubilee* (1966), Octavia Butler's *Kindred* (1979), Sherley Williams's *Dessa Rose* (1986), Toni Morrison's *Beloved* (1987), Charles Johnson's *Middle Passage* (1990), Barry Unsworth's *Sacred Hunger* (1992) and *The Quality of Mercy* (2010), Lorene Cary's *The Price of a Child* (1995), Edward P. Jones's *The Known World* (2003), Marie-Elena John's *Unburnable* (2006), and Isabelle Allende's *Island Beneath the Sea* (2011) are worthy of our notice. Each of these novels imaginatively takes up the era of the enslavement of Africans in the Americas and, in doing so, represents the genre's remarkable persistence. But what accounts for this particular preoccupation? Slavery's origin story has a shackle that shifts its shape, but not its grasp.

Public Fictions, Private Facts

My consideration of how legal and literary narratives intersect is particularly attentive to a theory of origins. The origins are constitutionally and legislatively provoked narratives of identity that emerged from a nation that had determined the ways in which it would be ruled and subsequently bound by law. A critical exchangeability between citizenship and personhood became a foundational principle of the nation's body politic and eventually composed a critical facet of its literary fiction.

The focused readings of black literary fiction in this book reveal the substantive consequences of a utilitarian and ultimately intersectional polity between law and literature. My quite intentional critical practice derives from my consideration of what it is that ultimately emerges as the theoretical imperative that invigorates race as a persistently viable construction in U.S. cultures. Law is responsible for blood rule, a *contingent* legalism of the biologic that is legally sustained, oddly in an effort to make the association between conduct and color illegal. A brief example may be helpful in explaining this seemingly difficult association.

In late 2010, Rudolph Byrd and Henry Louis Gates explained how renowned Harlem Renaissance writer Jean Toomer "passed" as a white man.[9] Their trail of evidence began with legal documents—marriage licenses filled out by Toomer where he identified his race as white, or where he allowed a clerk to make that notation without objection. In other words, Toomer's four score years of celebrity as a black writer chronicling the Negro Renaissance was directly contradicted by legal documentation that he was responsible for filing during the same era of his literary renown. Is the public fact of his celebrated black literariness different from the legal instantiation of his private white identity? Was he a black writer of the Harlem Renaissance or the white husband of Marjorie Content? In what ways does this matter? The complex terrain of legally cognizable racial identity and culturally constructed black arts is illustrated in the complicated artistry that can produce a black writer ("make a poet black . . .") and a legal, white spouse as the same person, and then find a way to "bid him sing."[10]

This slender incident of identity is exemplary of the way in which race is legally bound. It has been an omnipresent reality of black life in the United States and it became a uniquely nationalized condition of personhood. Racial identity was an imposed and prescriptive legalism that controlled access to legal citizenship as the idea of identity itself evolved into something odd enough to fuel a literary imagination. The federal constitution of race in the United States as well as its subsequent fugitivity — its evasions from legal control — stand as evidence in the malleable associations attached to its appearance. This complex relational problematic produces the stuff of fiction.

My argument is consistent with Lauren Berlant's understanding that the America that "dominates [Nathaniel Hawthorne's] represented relation to his activity, his knowledge, his affect [and] his very body . . . is primarily textual."[11] This perspective of textuality is corporeal. Its institutional and legal corporatism sharpens my focus on a nationally engaged fiction of citizenship. The association between citizenship and personhood is evident in the structure of the social, the practice of law, and the composition of narrative. Critical to this association is the apparent and fundamental premise that our national fictions (the ideas we embody regarding race) and the nation's literary fictions (how we enact our socialities) have legal histories. I am interested in the presumptive integrity of the association—specifically in whatever it is that sustains the intimate intersectionality between legal citizenship and black personhood. What seems less predictable but nonetheless exemplary is the way in which U.S. literary fictions illustrate this association in texts that resonate with the effects of the regulatory dimensions of U.S. jurisprudence. This includes both the effort to determinatively regulate race and to apply legal consequences when there is a failure to do so.

Consider, for example, a novel like Toni Morrison's *Beloved* that reproduces a fugitive imagination in the character of the ghostly persona of Beloved.[12] Beloved is sometimes a ghost, but at other times she is a living presence—Sethe's dead daughter returned from the grave. The narrative seeks to find a reasonable place for her ephemeral presence in the story at the same time that it attempts to sustain the efforts of a community of freed and fugitive blacks whose lives are just a breath away and a river across from slavery. The enforcement and recapture threatened in the Fugitive Slave Act instantiated an always present and brutally policed potential; a consistent tear at the vulnerable threads of the community. At the same time, the ghostly Beloved begins her frightful inhabitation as fabric—begging the association with the metaphor 'the fabric of our nation': "a white dress knelt down next to her mother and had its sleeve around her mother's [Sethe's] waist" (39). Sethe, shaken by the visible presence of the daughter she murdered finds her own legal and ethical vulnerability shaped against a relational and now a troublingly visible metaphysics.

We might also recall the worry of John's mother in James Baldwin's *Go Tell It on the Mountain*.[13] In a playful yet deadly serious exchange with her delinquent son Roy, he tells her "You think that all that's in the world is jails and churches?" (Baldwin 1970, 23). Roy's focus on this locative binary—two oppositional but similarly regulatory sites in which his mother's practiced imagination allows her to visualize her children's potential—illustrates the disciplined ethic attached to black lives. Both law and religion ("jails and churches") depend on a prior and a conferred authority. Baldwin's novel acknowledges these similarly knotted potentials. One of the sons (Roy) leaves home and is seriously wounded in a violent altercation with white hoodlums that foreshadows his tragically colored future. He may as well have been Lydia attempting to fight back against Mann's violence; or, fictively, Richard Wright's fearful and fated Bigger Thomas in *Native Son*. In Baldwin's autobiographical first novel, John — Roy's brother — enters the church giving further credence to their mother's predictive binary.

Go Tell It on the Mountain suggests a precedent in the literary history of the black novel that can be related to Morrison's configuration of an alternative to the consequential collision of slave law. It at least augurs the promise of unbounded liberalism of her spiritual/religious authority. Morrison's Baby Suggs, Holy, herself a fugitive from the Kentucky plantation, offers her daughter-in-law refuge in her Ohio home. She was the community's spiritual leader who led sermons in a clearing near her home, but she finds the task of mediating the physical and psychic harms of the past or naming the bodily harms, giving them a reverence ("love your hands, your mouth . . .") through a synecdochic dismemberment, too much for even the generous spirituality she offers to the community gathered in the clearing. Baby Suggs retreats from her public role to a private spirit-space that allows her to spend the last of her days pondering color. It seems a final refuge that makes way and room for the liberated creativity she would have practiced had not the psychic threat of return and recapture loomed larger than her spiritual will. She retreats to a private landscape — both the least and the most textural site that might manifest her loss — playing with bits of untethered fabrics, remnants of her frayed imagination and imagined liberalism.

Imaginative liberalism suggests a contingent relationship between creativity and the potential of autonomy. Because both are dependent on personhood, their potential depends on the vitality (indeed, the viability and visibility) of the body that would enable that imaginary. If a person's capacity for autonomous act is constrained at any level, but particularly at the level of the legibility or cognizability, then that metaphysical knot of being and becoming—one always constitutive of the other—is inevitably contingent. Certainly Sethe's home, 124 Bluestone Road, holds no sanctuary. It is haunted and vulnerable. The tyranny and terror of white law comes into it like a home invasion. "They came in her yard anyway . . . the whitefolks had tired her out at last" (Morrison 1987, 207).

Simile as Precedent

Property and contract are emblematically critical doctrines that actively constitute and consistently invigorate the idea of race and the doctrine of law. They effectively bind the development of fictions' black characters and society's black citizens to a legally inscribed personhood. These are doctrines that, for example, make Morrison's Sethe unable to divest herself of the fear in her legal *being* as an escaped slave at the same time she tries to shape herself as a mother. It is the kind of dilemma that prompted Ntozake Shange to write, "bein alive & bein a woman & bein colored is a metaphysical dilemma / I havent conquered yet."[14] Sethe's private and personal selves are legally and morally incompatible. She intrinsically appreciates the appeal of Baby-Suggs's emotional escape. In fact, she nearly succumbs to it herself at the novel's end when Paul D. interferes with the intentionality of her dying. But at the novel's beginning, Sethe tries to teach her surviving daughter Denver something different, warning her that the pathological detritus of the past does not necessarily stay in the past. She uses words, but her reach is metaphysical. In legal terms, she might be talking about precedent or, as formally known in the law—*stare decisis et non quieta movere*—to stand by decisions and not disturb the undisturbed, when she explains:

> I was talking about time. It's so hard for me to believe in it. Some things go. Pass on. Some things just stay. I used to think it was my rememory. You know. Some things you forget. Other things you never do. But it's not. Places, places are still there. If a house burns down, it's gone, but the place—the picture of it—stays, and not just in my rememory, but

out there, in the world. What I remember is a picture floating around out there outside of my head. I mean even if I don't think it, even if I die, the picture of what I did, or knew, or saw is still out there. Right in the place where it happened. . . . Someday you be walking down the road and you hear something or see something going on . . . And you think it's you thinking it up . . . But no. It's when you bump into a re-memory that belongs to somebody else. (Morrison 1998, 46–47)

In the way that precedent contours jurisprudence, rememory — especially as instantiated memory of race — is a construct that retains its solidity and presence despite the passage of time.

Law is like rememory. It is the thing W. H. Auden suggested was what "all gardeners obey" in his 1941 poem, "Law Like Love."[15] Black fiction's concerns with rights and citizenship, and what and how material gains and personal characteristics evolve, make, and retain substance, are the discipline's sustained interrogatives. Despite the ways in which the Constitution might clarify these matters, when black writers "play in the dark," rights somehow seem less like law than a fugitive emanation — Auden's "love we can't compel or fly / Like love we often weep / Like love we seldom keep." Auden's suggestion of the provocative similarity between the two is a useful comparison for the narrative associations that contextualize this book. Interestingly, when Auden wrote, "Law Like Love" he was in transition from residence in Britain to America. It is a navigable interlude that might reasonably serve to introduce our recollection of English common law traditions that are evident in American legal systems.

These English legal traditions are apparent in Kantian claims regarding the moral normativity of natural law, especially with regard to the intimate association between rights and personhood. I think this literary history especially provocative, because in the United States the physical constitution of personhood is precisely what is at stake in contemporary as well as earlier black fictions as much as it is a recurrent matter of law. The twinned sociolegal evolution of these frames is a vital contemporary element of legal narratives and moral theory. And it is not inconsequential that each is sutured to the idea of rights. The right to property, or the right one has to enter into contract, or the right to bear witness is not casual verbiage. These rights are implicit to the Jeffersonian ideal of citizenship.

Neither is it inconsequential that these rights become both more complicated and frustratingly perverse when race matters. The rights to enter into a contract, to own property, and to bear witness (proffer evidence) were fundamental in the framing of the Constitution. Each was specifically attached to citizenship that, for blacks, was first described as three-fifths of all other *persons*. This condition posed a legal conundrum that meant one's humanity or personhood was negotiated through the constitution of citizenship. Its constitution is evident in contemporary legal arguments that there are nonhuman entities, corporations, that have the legal standing and rights of a citizen, as well as the particular argument relevant to this text, that the U.S. Constitution still retains the potential to legislatively support the making (and unmaking) of persons—and even to designate some of these persons as nonhuman.[16] A lay understanding of rights almost always extends from these foundational principles that are for some appropriate appeals to the moral reasoning attached to human(e) normativity. And yet these rights in particular were confounded when the Constitution, an appropriate legacy to Locke's second treatise of government, acknowledged them as foundational to the rights of man (where ownership of one's own self was specifically noted). When attached to the formation of U.S. personhood the idea of rights codified national particularities that would sustain legally cognizable differences between human beings. These differences were essential to the formation of a national economy that depended on disparate bodies, and the law—always interested in a public policy that would sustain the nation—cooperated in their creation.[17] The law expended significant energy in determining and renegotiating what these particularities meant, whether it was attached to color or blood, especially with regard to how these particularities might interact with the presumptive natural right to citizenry for white (heterosexual) males.

Noticing the social evolution of legal rights as they have been incorporated into fictive narratives of racial identity is a critical interest of this text. But as important is the persistence of their relational evolution. It is not unreasonable to imagine that a fundamental right, like the right to property, would eventually disassociate itself from its origin. Humans as legally protected property dissolved with the abolition of slavery. Nevertheless, and despite the dislocation that memory would seem to argue for, some legally inscribed memory of origin is particularly critical to the history of evolution and figural attachments of U.S. property law. Matters of property continue to reify their relationship to Justinian code—wherein property was understood as the right to use and abuse a thing, within the boundaries of law. Laws that regulate abortion or that regulate organ donation or patent stem cells consistently engage an ethic that is conceptually related to John Locke's dictum that our "lives, liberties and estates are our property because we own our bodies."[18] Clearly there was a decided appeal in this consideration for those who wrote our Constitution, even while there was that problematic issue of who "our" would be in a nation where the difference of bodies was visibly critical. The Constitution's representation clause was designed to address this detachment of our philosophies from the nation's diverse bodies. It settled on the peculiar but expedient and useable logic that if there was not a full body, it was not entitled to full personhood. Although much of the discussion of this clause engages who shall count as a citizen, it also mattered not simply for representational privilege, but it reflected the critical philosophical interest we had in addressing the appealing Lockean consideration of who might be included in the ownership of "our" bodies.

Although slavery is a long-standing artifact of cultural histories around the world, the association of black bodies to enslavement and to "blackness" as vulnerable to this particular biologic constructionism fundamentally altered the critical association of property to the idea, or a (critical to the idea of property) potential of alienability and consequently queered the way in which U.S. laws might evolve with regard to as archaic a notion as property. Locke could easily imagine a personal "we own our bodies" potential as long as the "we" could be disentangled from the visibly distinct bodies that populated the newly composed Americas. However, when identity matters—and this is true for gender and sexuality as well as race—the legal origin never wanders too far from the substance of the claim. This is why a perversely paired historic ideology of rights that determines the use and abuse of property as a logical, or a suprasensible, regulation could even arbitrarily follow the regard of bodies as property. It took an imaginable liberalism to do so.

Property, Contract, and Evidentiary Values

Two legal doctrines attach to the principle of property law and frame the readings that compose the chapters that follow this introduction. I select them because they are consistent with constitutional protections as well as its presumptive liberties. They form the basis of our idea of citizenship and assure the patterns of its practice.

Understanding the idea of geographies as sites of imaginative freedom as well as historical cartographies, legal precedents, and literary bookmarks have helped as I've selected which of the many diverse literary fictions from the tradition of African American letters I should include in this manuscript. These guidelines have helped me make those difficult selections.

First, I've used black fiction from the twentieth and twenty-first centuries because these have been the years when legislation and specific legal principles (levels of scrutiny, equal protection) that address the issues of race and rights have been especially prolific. The genre of neo–slave narratives stands as particularly provocative evidence of the dense literary and legal landscapes that matter well past their historical era. Novels from this tradition are powerfully illustrative of the persistence of this lingering history.

Second, I am particularly interested in intentionally literary fiction rather than genre fiction that reaches a more popular market. Although my argument is indeed that nearly all African American fiction inevitably engages some dimension of the legal is absolutely applicable to the wide range of U.S. black fictions, and my sincere hope is that interested readers test this presumption by considering how a wider variety of black fiction fits within this thesis, my interests for this text settle with those that (1) commit to a literary aesthetic ahead of those markers apparent in more formulaic conventions of genre (romance, detective, mystery, etc.) and (2) have an earned familiarity as classic black literary fiction. As a consequence of the first matter of artistry, I've selected texts where a reader is more likely to find the legal less a consequence of plot than it is a scalar variable of its composition. And the natural development of that criteria combined with the secondary interest in a familiar tradition of black classic literary fiction means that I have used novels by authors like James Baldwin, David Bradley, Ralph Ellison, Ernest Gaines, Charles Johnson, Nella Larsen, Toni Morrison, Walter Mosley, Gloria Naylor, Ann Petry, Alice Walker, and Richard Wright, whose works engage extraordinary depth and capacity and whose imaginative texts have earned the designation as classic literary fiction to illustrate the arguments within this book. I encourage readers to consider for themselves the ways in which these writers and others I have not named here also imagine the convergence of the literary with the legal frames of property, contract, and evidence.

The format of the book follows three critical legal frames and, in addition to a variety of fiction and references to legal cases, I bring a particular legal narrative to each of the chapters and use that narrative to link the literary references and the legal framework.

The substantive claims of *property* are the focus of chapter 1, and it is this book's touchstone, nearly a ghostly inhabitation haunting the black body and consequently a persistent recollection in the chapters that follow. Property's penumbral presence is deeply complicated because of the legal origins that give U.S. law the potential to make and unmake persons. The legal history of people as property is a constitutional origin story that has made notions and designations of property invade every attempt to emerge from the legal thicket of a proscriptive black identity. Judge Ruffin gestures to this history in *State v. Mann*, noting in the text of the decision the struggle between "the feelings of man and the duty of the magistrate"

(264) and the way in which the "subject" [Lydia] is "doomed in [her] own person, to live without knowledge, and without the capacity, to make anything his own" (266). "Anything" includes personhood, which is the property of the owner, rather than one's self. The way in which literature plays with that ontological confusion is evident in Charles Johnson's *Middle Passage*. When and how can we discuss a question of ontology if its very constitution, indeed its substance, always and already insists that the origin of personhood consistently matters? It is a provocative thicket that explains why fiction has found the problem so compelling and how the genre of the neo–slave narrative, whether Charles Johnson's *Middle Passage* or Morrison's *Beloved*, continue to have such marketability centuries past the era of slavery.

This book focuses on the issue of contract in Gloria Naylor's *Linden Hills* (1985), a novel that depends on the narratives that emerge from the legal issues of property in a neighborhood that is circled with intestate successions determining the ownership of homes and the placement of certain families at varying levels of a social hierarchy. Property matters locate and ground the narrative in Toni Morrison's *Sula* (1973), which has as its most consistent image an oddly configured house that becomes a chaotic sanctuary for its residents (a theme she returns to in *Paradise* [1998]) as well as a threat. It's the place where Eva burns her drug-addicted grandson Plum.

In chapter 2 laws of *evidence* (including the necessary components of witness and testimony) incorporate the textual substance of fiction as well as its characterizations. I trace their appearance in fictions as widely divergent as Ann Petry's "The Witness" to the epistles in Alice Walker's *The Color Purple* (1982) and Ellison's *Invisible Man* (1952), where a letter serves as both a proffered contract and as evidence of the "nigger boy's" origins. Admissible evidence as the legal standard binds narratives of property and contract. It stands as the evident physicality of a claim in the person of the body who makes it or in the *materia* that allows property and contract to emerge as fundamental rights. Two legal cases of enslaved Africans aboard ships—the *Antelope* and the *Amistad*—provide the legal history that allows the necessary narrative complications of evidentiary bound-aries.

In chapter 3, I focus on parameters of *contract*. I consider the narra-tive exposition of the legal and moral knottiness of a promise, the poten-tial of economic commerce, and the viability of a private right. Only in the United States, where persons were woven into a legal construction as commerce, would the commercial consequence form a legal question with regard to whether a promise to a black person had cognizable stand-ing (much less moral obligation) and a right to the insular protections of private law. The private laws of testament and succession assured that race mattered. Contract is the embedded narrative of marriage in Nella Larsen's novella *Passing* (1929). The Rhinelander case mentioned briefly in that novel frames the legal issues considered in this chapter. The im-plicit laws of testimony that that case protected formulate the baseline that structures the legal agreement between the "property" owner and the wealthy industrialist who occupies the basement prison in Walter Mosley's *The Man in My Basement* (2004).

In this book's epilogue—"When and Where 'All the Dark-Glass Boys' Enter"—I explore ways in which majority American writers engage these paradigmatic issues of law as well, albeit with a difference. This is a book about America's literary histories, and although its focus is fiction by black writers it seemed as important to return here to the nudge from Morri-son's *Playing in the Dark*, in its insistence that those racialized imaginar-ies are a necessary aspect of the "critical geography" of the *nation's* litera-tures.[19] These geographies are also the spaces of a national imaginary, a metaphysics that connects Morrison's notion of rememory to Foucault's exploration of heterotopia. There is a compelling argument that law is the physical mirror, the actual object that makes the heterotopic site pos-sible. For this perspective of geography, this chapter also relies on British novelist Barry Unsworth's engagement with infamous histories regarding the slave trade between the Americas and Britain as a critical illustration of the origin of British common law that was the precedent in U.S. law and the reach of the slave narrative across the middle passage. Fiction by classic writers of American literary canon, Mark Twain, Harper Lee, William Faulkner, Scott Fitzgerald, and Flannery O'Connor support this legal jouissance and give compelling evidence of the ways in which law and race become dependent literary bedfellows. "When and Where 'All the Dark-Glass Boys' Enter," suggests the ways in which our national literatures as well as our national traditions have a critical legal composition.

Although each chapter relies on the particular foci described above, the astute reader will notice there are inevitable intersections. Property claims connect to evidence (Eva's house burns and a drug addicted grandson lies dead inside); evidentiary matters might well depend on contractual obligations, and those could easily depend on ownership and standing. In *State v. Mann* the question might have been whether or not Lydia is a person in the eyes of the law who has rights to her body's protection from harm. But instead the legal question was framed by the presumption that Lydia *was* property and therefore what property rights would matter in reference to the owner's claims. It was a judicial choice that certainly depended on the social as much as the legal. Nevertheless, the legal effectively subordinates the social. In that era, and in the eyes of the court, Lydia was invisible as a rights-bearing person. In fact, she was constitutionally only partially a person and had no proximity at all to citizenship. Her owners, however, were the ones with cognizably viable claims. This point is critical to understanding the way in which law devises or composes a legal fiction in order to adjudicate. Law makes it necessary to disaggregate the social intersectionalities and paradoxes. Judicial duty requires clarification of the legal question that will constitute the case narrative (admissible evidence) and the ruling. And in doing so, it effectively erases the standing of any penumbral questions. However, in literature, it is precisely the author's ability to play with this complexity that makes for the compelling tangles of fiction. Legal determinations may be arbitrary but they are nonetheless concretizing. Literary imaginations liberate and allow, indeed encourage, the leak of one to the other. This critical intersectionality is inevitable and notable.

Even though American jurisprudence has shown itself willing to engage, determine, and amend questions of gender and race, U.S. literatures took up similar questions but without the necessity that the law has for resolution and fixity. In fact, literature's openness to conflict and its practiced interest in complexity and ease with the obscure kept the pretense of legal resolution from being the sociocultural panacea its regulations would offer. The legal fiction of race and identity was the liberal imaginary, the terrain of literature. Literatures in the United States have consistently reflected and creatively engaged America's shifting social judgments on questions of rights that the law has arguably settled, or at least that the law has sought to provide, through various rulings, with a substantive judicial framework for resolution. However, in the (fugitive) hands of creative writers, the principles attached to rights become malleable fictions that depended on the bodies that are constituted as its primary actors—its characters. This book will argue that black folk made for particularly complex literary characters precisely because of the way in which their very bodies were out(side of)law. However, in the hands of judicial actors, the principles are similarly malleable when race complicates what the law might otherwise settle. Property rights engaged testamentary freedoms. (Can a black woman inherit property if she is property?) The ability to transfer wealth—the economic foundation of this nation—brought with it the necessity of exchanging bodies from one generation to the next. Private property was racial and sexual economy.[20] Private law made certain that testamentary freedoms were embodied or corporeal before they were legally cognizable. This is a messy legal landscape, and we see its effects in the contradictory, repetitive, inconsistent laws regarding race in the United States. While law just kept trying to sort it out, literature— especially that written by black writers—would out the inconsistencies, explore the lacunae, and weigh the unanticipated accompaniments embedded in racialized narratives that made a fiction of the law.

ONE

The Claims of Property

On Being and Belonging

Are they men? Then make them citizens. Are they property?
Why, then, is no other property included?
— Gouveneur Morris, *James Madison, The Debates in the Several*
State Conventions of the Adoption of the Federal Constitution, vol. 5, 1787

Home—an anxiety of belonging.
— Toni Morrison, "Home," 1997

The foundational principles of governance that have an intimate association with property can be found in a penultimate version of the Declaration of Independence. The judgment eventually expressed in the Declaration regarding the familiar triumvirate — "life, liberty and the pursuit of happiness" — actually had its generation in an earlier document, The Virginia Declaration of Rights, composed by George Mason and unanimously adopted by the Virginia Convention of Delegates on June 12, 1776. Mason's declaration contended "that all men are by nature equally free and independent, and have certain inherent rights, of which, when they enter into a state of society, they cannot, by any compact, deprive or divest their posterity; namely, the enjoyment of life and liberty, *with the means of acquiring and possessing property*, and pursuing and obtaining happiness and safety."[1]
Legal scholar Cheryl Harris has written perhaps the most provocative

and critically compelling essay identifying the inherent propertied value in whiteness.[2] For Harris the nomination of whiteness as a tangible thing like property invests it with an inalienability and control that was fundamentally proprietary. This value came to direct legal resolutions that protected claims made on the behalf of white citizens. In the United States slavery attached to the necessities that accompanied our nation's formation. Its identitarian evolution was a matter of pragmatism that evolved into both a structure and philosophy of discrimination. Harris's claim is that American legal systems were constituted in ways that made them innately and vigorously protective of whiteness as a value — something with the commercial attributes of property that attached to one's personhood. Her argument not only explains the coordinate evolution of property and persons, but it clarifies the persistence of its vexed commodification. The nation's laws sustained what might otherwise have been an ephemeral if not merely a legal value. Harris's essay is a strikingly creative and, in my judgment, a correct reading of often convoluted legal cases in early America that twisted their way through laws of property and inheritance to make certain that white persons and the national state that depended on them would maintain their privilege. They did so by an inordinate focus on the limits and nature of blackness — in decisions as defamatory as *Dred Scott v. Sandford* and as (arguably) normalizing as the Civil Rights amendments.[3]

One way of understanding how quickly the nation came to invest in a regulatory discrimination between the kinds of persons native to and those who immigrated to these American shores is to consider the way in which religion was among the first identitarian interests expressed in state laws. Those earliest identitarian-based Virginia codes determined that Christianity would be the identity that determined the difference between those who would be slaves and those liberated from this assignation. Some critical conditionality of enslavement was the variable in a system that persisted, at least through "badges and incidents of slavery" centuries past its legal practice.[4] During the colonial era, the systematic shift that would distinguish servitude from legal slavery followed the need for the

English to have a consistent population of workers. As an example, consider the way in which the 1705 Virginia General Assembly documented the transformation and clarified the evolved status of blacks and Indians.

> All servants imported and brought into the Country . . . who were not Christians in their native Country . . . shall be accounted and be slaves. All Negro, mulatto and Indian slaves within this dominion . . . shall be held to be real estate. If any slave resist his master . . . correcting such slave, and shall happen to be killed in such correction . . . the master shall be free of all punishment . . . as if such accident never happened.[5]

The statutes not only affirmed slave status, but they instantiated a social necessity to confirm and solidify that distinction. That need would be evident in law and in society during the centuries that followed. It was a social shift that extended not only to persons brought into this country but was to become their progeny's legacy. Virginia's slave codes extended to any child borne of a mother who was enslaved.

The practice of the new republic would mirror the textual history of property's foundational ideology as a symbiotic accompanying reference to the construction of the nation, an ideology that was specifically attached to the color of the nation's citizens. Blackness and whiteness gained legal visibility. That identitarian focus, not unanticipated since religious identity was foremost in the minds of the earliest settlers as the ethical measure that distinguished them from the country they left, lasted as long as it was practical. But as chattel slavery expanded to support the growing economic dependence on imported labor, national origin became the more expedient and commercially profitable category to designate a person's potential in this country. One interesting version of the unique American nature of that distinction and the problems that inhered is that persons who came to the United States from Great Britain, who would be understood to be nonwhite in this nation's parlance, easily appreciated the value the United States placed on white identity (and earlier, on Christianity) as a means to access. Despite their skin color, these persons would argue for whiteness as their appropriate legal category despite an appearance that might at least ambiguate the claim. As late as 1923, in a claim by an "Aryan Indian" to the explicit value attached to U.S. whiteness, the Supreme Court of the United States ruled that for the purposes of being classified as an American citizen "Aryans" whose origin was the continent of India were not to be considered white persons.[6]

What kind of sociolegal environment made whiteness a normative value that so easily attached to the right to property? The era's jurisprudence made certain that property was a contingent value. Social practices, including the rape of enslaved women and the unique differentiation from familial "ownership" of children from those encounters, led to a plethora of confusing and contradictory regulations, often dependent on the state of origin, that noted blood quantum or patrilineal versus matrilineal status (as enslaved or free) as the determinative legal category. Courts developed odd and perverse racial reasons—With whom does the person associate with in the neighborhood? What do teachers consider as the child's racial identity? What was the claim when a marriage was performed? What would be the impact on children who might stand to inherit from the estate? As to the matter of the individual, the standards varied from skin color, ancestry, or some idiosyncratic variable.[7]

It is not difficult to imagine a contemporary legacy of slave codes, or to anticipate they would have some visible persistence in the decades immediately past the era of slavery. In fact, the most reasonable site to explore for the intersections of law and literature happen at this juncture in U.S. legal and social histories, when the manipulation of a history of British common law shifted in order to incorporate the bodies that became commerce. The consequent confusion between persons and property—where a person might act outside of the contingencies of property—make for narratives that recall the law's corporeal enactment, its intimacy with regard to bodies caught in legal definitions of slaves, real estate, citizens, and persons. The very embodiment of law, its ability to incorporate, becomes its legal conceit. And because this is true, it is particularly important not to skip the moment in U.S. legal history when persons were absolutely property—before they were not. William Blackstone's *Commentaries on the Laws of England* states the precedent of U.S. legal philosophies regarding property. Blackstone wrote, "There is nothing which so generally strikes the imagination . . . as the right of property; or that sole and despotic dominion which one man exercises over the external things of the world."[8] That legal imagination would be literature's playing field. The very potential of a fugitive, or an outlaw, acting in a way that suggests a credible synthesis between a human person and an entity like property gives fiction its extraordinary potential and makes legal precedent a visible cartography of that geography of identity. Little wonder that law continues to analyze and parse its own intent with regard to corporate personalities.

The legal history began in the early 1800s when the Trustees of Dartmouth College successfully applied the contract clause (the subject of chapter 3 of this book) to their argument that their charter gave them a corporate identity, affirmed the sanctity of contract, and protected them from a legislative effort to shift their status from private to public. In *Trustees of Dartmouth College v. Woodward*, Chief Justice John Marshall explained the court's understanding of the college's identity and established what would become the landmark precedent for the substantive potential of nonhuman persons. Notably, Marshall's decision speaks of personhood as something invested with "properties." He wrote: "A corporation is an artificial being, invisible, intangible, and existing only in contemplation of law. Being the mere creature of law, it possesses only those properties that the charter of its creation confers on it, either expressly, or as incidental to its very existence."[9] Marshall's judgment repeats the idea of an authority to declare and attach properties that would make, or unmake, one's personhood.

The Capital in Question

The intersecting relationship between property and contract is critical to the convoluted narrative of Charles Johnson's neo–slave narrative *Middle Passage*.[10] The novel's main character is a freed black man, Rutherford, who is returned to slavery on a ship ironically and emblematically named the *Republic*. Once the ship's harrowing voyage of rebellion and mysticisms is complete, and when Rutherford finds himself back in New Orleans once again holding onto the papers that would legally document his claim to freedom and regain his status as a freed man that the ship's voyage unmoored, the novel seems to have returned to a safe harbor. However, nothing in that document assured his survival, whether he was at sea or on land. At sea, maritime rules interfered, and coupled with the unruliness of the ship's passage, the absent ethics of its mission, and the confusion of authorities that attempted to maintain some semblance of control, the ship was no place for documentary authority.

Middle Passage depends greatly on the legal and extralegal performances and enforcement of slavery. It did not matter that Rutherford had the papers to prove it. In black hands, documents are contingent. Rutherford makes that point clear on the novel's first page: "In 1829 when I arrived from southern Illinois—a newly freed bondman, my papers in an old portmanteau, a gift from my master" (1, 2). That distinction of identity—he was no longer a slave—was a critical nomination toward an identitarian permanence. But it was unfortunately attached to the ongoing ontological formation of race. Although the papers might confer freedom, his visibly dark body argued for his enslavement, assuring that there would always be a contest between the two. But since race was not fixed, neither was his status. Consider the syntactic ambiguity embedded in Johnson's sentence. It leaves oblique which thing was the gift: was it the portmanteau, or the papers? If this was *donatio mortis causa*—a deathbed gift—it is, by the traditions of English common laws that were the basis of U.S. jurisprudence, legally inalienable. And yet, to make Rutherford a gift of himself would also establish him as a legal person, able to receive an inalienable gift, even though there was a constitutional clause that denied him the citizenship that attends personhood. The era's contradictory interplay between persons and citizens is as tantalizingly vague in law as it was in society, and Johnson's Rutherford has a confoundingly peripatetic nature that exemplifies that instability. Once aboard the *Republic*, the authority those papers might have obtained in port leveraged little of their heft in adjudicating his status. On the open seas, he is vulnerable.

Middle Passage explores the rich potential of the dislocation of a destabilized property, and it engages the fugitive imagination both as liberal legalism and as fictive entanglement. But it is *the personification of property* that gives the narrative its persistence. Property as personhood runs perilously close to constitutional doctrine that would notice a "badge or incident" of slavery as a reasonable indication of bias.[11] Rutherford's portmanteau is a reformulation of the letter carried in a briefcase by Ellison's *Invisible Man* that instructs whoever reads it to "keep this nigger boy running."[12] Clearly Johnson's novel depends on the creativity attached to the fiction of freedom implicit in the paradox between stability and flight. But it does so by engaging the vexed terrain of the intersections between personhood, citizenship, and rights that the law has placed into play into the discourse of this book's focus. Nevertheless, given the era of its publication, a place may be claimed for it as a novel that is postmodern in its execution, and like Ellison's *Invisible Man* it can claim a kinship that goes beyond the disciplined genres of twentieth-century literature.

The critical question that shapes this text asks why matters about personhood, slavery, and identity would continue to exert such profound narrative energy long past the era of slavery. Johnson's novel is fiction of the late twentieth century. And although the close but focused readings of fiction here do consider these neo–slave narratives, my interest in doing so is to highlight the ways in which questions of property and personhood structure the fictions that follow, even those that do not depend on slavery as their literary site.

Personhood and citizenship have a constitutional boundedness that makes one a legal version of the other. However, there is also a clear and compelling history in the constitution of persons attaching to one's humanity. This ontological tangle becomes the stuff of fictions even as the relatedness between personhood and conferred citizenship becomes settled law. The law continues its legal fixes—with legislation in the 1860s and in the 1960s that repaired rights not yet fully enjoyed. It deployed affirmative actions and varying forms of scrutiny to adjudicate claims regarding racial inequities. Strict scrutiny—the highest judicial level of interpretive regard—is called for in claims regarding racial disparities. In its consistent return to the matter of race and rights, U.S. law has effectively reified the legal and normative questions regarding race, identity, and selfhood. Because of the earliest constitutional language, the legal history in the matter of persons become claims of property as well—are you a person or something owned? Do you have an "immutable" identity? How does the value of a thing attach to its utility, and how does law recognize shifting social values and utilities?

Finally, there is the question that indicates the intimate relationship between privacy and personhood: What about a person is inviolate and how can that inviolability stand if the law must recognize the distinction that makes a difference retain its potential for a compelling fiction?[13] The tidy resolution seemingly available through law becomes the valuable terrain for legal fictions to engage a literary imagination fully invested with the attendant contradictions, complexities, and habits of precedent and tradition that have followed the evolution of racialized legal claims. Law retains its acts of certainty and resolution, and despite its axiomatic character, looks to fabricate a regulatory elegance. Of course, this makes it ideal terrain for a fiction, and the perplexity of problems that are identity based makes this a particularly compelling landscape for black fiction because the constitution of its characters as racialized come to depend on a consistent legal reincarnation that emerges as justification of the distinctions. From the era of enslavement through this day, race matters precisely because the law will not release it. As a consequence, the law turns on the fearsome potential of illegibility and illegitimacy. As long as these are properties of a body—legalisms will readily attach.

Johnson's novel is deeply embedded with the character and quality of racial belonging. Isadora, who wanted to be his wife, actually turns him over to a slaver. Rutherford's fractured logic initially sees this consequence as a lesser evil than entering into the contract of marriage with her. From Rutherford's perspective that potentially (extra)legal opportunity was another potential imprisonment. But his personhood is so loosely and contingently configured that his consignment to the *Republic*, a ship that would endure a bloody resurrection, that would unmoor his identity as a freed black man and encapsulate a darkly threatening mystical evidence that would literally expose the horror of Middle Passage slave routes, would nearly be his undoing. The narrative's necessary coherence in the face of these oft-times incoherently complex and competing stories comes from the regulation implicit in this thick legal embeddedness — the proffered contract of marriage, the documentary, textual evidence of his freedom (the papers he carried), and the competing laws of maritime rule that regulated on- and offshore events and conduct. Johnson's story succeeds because of this narrative knot of jurisprudence and the web of evidence that binds it. But the novel's coherence falls apart precisely when the law no longer has a mooring place, neither in the Americas nor in the bowels of the ship where a mysterious monstrosity threatens the foundations of everything above it. A rebellion that has at its core a battle over (and arguably "by") commerce and capital destabilizes the *Republic*.

Rutherford is sometimes enslaved, sometimes free, sometimes a snitch, at other times a leader of the rebellion. His crisis of identity is as chaotic as the ship's failed voyage and is ultimately characteristic of contingent legalism. His is a postmodernist identitarian effacement that quite easily finds itself reflected in Fredric Jameson's argument that "postmodernism in culture — whether apologia or stigmatization — is also at one and the same time, and *necessarily*, an implicitly or explicitly political stance on the nature of multinational capitalism."[14] There seems no status that does not reify the predicaments of his increasing associations and affiliations with the ship's property — its enslaved cargo. Baleka, a child of one of the captured Allmuseri, is (like Morrison's Beloved) as much a haunt of that potential humanity as she is a tease of its inaccessibility. Johnson ties Rutherford's emerging humanism with his concern for the child: "Whenever Baleka is out of my sight I am worried. If she bruises herself I feel bruised. Night and day I pray all will go well for her, even after I am gone. Sometimes she drives me to distraction . . . if she is quiet for too long, I worry about that as well" (195). These are certainly parental feelings, but they are as well the concerns of an owner. When it comes to black bodies and value, the distinctions turned on their assigned value.

Systems of U.S. slavery meant that whatever relations slave masters would have with enslaved women, none of them could face a threat to their fundamental rights of property. No indentured servant's child nor enslaved would inherit the social or legal status of a white father. Because slavery could be passed on, and because it became distinctive to persons who were not white—in that era Indigenous Americans or Negroes—its embodiment became as much identity as it was status. Claims of race and class were sutured to the claims of and nature of property. For whites, the histories in common law rules of testamentary freedoms attached to the mothers' status precisely because of the interests in keeping the progeny of enslaved-master relations as the property of the master rather than the legate of a father. It was, as Robert Reid-Pharr perceptively notes, a "domestic instability" that "ensure[d] the dynamic nature of the body/household dialectic in that it guarantees the production of irregular bodies." The irregularity is not only corporeal, it is legal. This was not just what Reid-Pharr notes as a "particularized set of *social* relations" but a complex and embedded architecture of legal relations as well.[15]

Little wonder that Toni Morrison could write such a compelling novel based on that legal execution of the idea of generation—*Beloved*—and include in it the narrative of how a mother's love could embrace infanticide in order to resist the law of generation that would make property of any child Sethe had. Her body mattered more than its geographies. Not only could she be reclaimed as property—as assured by the federal Fugitive Slave Act that applied across state borders—but her children would not be her own. Cheryl Harris's aforementioned essay explains the evolutionary intimacy between race and identity:

> Although the early colonists were cognizant of race, racial lines were neither consistently nor sharply delineated among or within all social groups. Captured Africans sold in the Americas were distinguished

from the population of indentured or bond servants — "unfree" white labor — but it was not an irrebuttable preoccupation that all Africans were "slaves," or that slavery was the only appropriate status for them. The distinction between African and white indentured labor grew, however, as decreasing terms of service were introduced for white bondservants. Simultaneously, the demand for labor intensified. . . . The construction of white identity and the ideology of racial hierarchy were intimately tied to the evolution and expansion of the system of chattel slavery. . . . The result was a classification system that "key[ed] official rules of descent to national origin" so that "[m]embership in the new social category of 'Negro' became itself sufficient justification for enslaveability." (Harris 1993, 278)

Legal investiture in maternal identity allowed critical patterns and codes of conduct to emerge. It was a pattern that preserved the commercial values inherent in paternity, privilege, and property. White plantation males could father children from their female slaves with the concurrent assurance that they would benefit both from an increase in their own property and be free from any concern that their progeny — whether males or females — would have any heritable claims. In the United States heritability meant that enslaved mothers had enslaved children and no claim to the value they represented to their owners. That experiential phenomenon came to be known as "one-drop" *rule* (of black blood) — statutes that were so fiercely nurtured that percentages of blood — blood quantum — led to a perverse vocabulary of legal identities (mulatto, quadroon, octoroon, and quintroon). Blood conveyed local sensibilities, carried legal consequence, and protected the propertied value of whiteness by its attention to even miniscule evidence of the taint of blackness. But the evolving legalisms that sutured families to histories of color as well as histories of race would continue to be an entailment. Literature certainly engages these issues of color and status, especially in the passing and tragic mulatto narratives, but instead of accepting a nuanced legal resolution, literature explores and resurrects the complications of identitarian-dependent fictions. Novels like Nella Larsen's *Passing* and *Quicksand* are compositions that depend on the constitution of race and color.

These vocabularies and practices represented the facts of social and legal customs and were clearly evident in the rule of society, and the processing of laws forced as much attention to color as they created ways to disclaim it. *Passing* was a novel of society manners similar in focus (the lives of young women and relationships developed in a tangle that foregrounded their lack of personal freedom) to something like Theodore Dreiser's *Sister Carrie*. But the narrative coherence of Larsen's *Passing* depended on a meticulous underbelly of antimiscegenation law. Even the brief mention in Larsen's text, "there was the Rhinelander case," reminds the reader that there are consequences to a marriage where race was (allegedly) a surprise revelation instead of a reliable presumption is a reference to the law's interest in matters of racial fraud (as was the issue in the Rhinelander matter).[16] Actual laws prohibiting intermarriage between races in a majority of states demonstrated governmental interest in racial identity.

Either the deception involved in passing for white or the interest in who is who in terms of racial identity was understood as a provocative text. This is the complex of fiction that Morrison's *Paradise* would take as its text.[17] In *Paradise*, the peculiarity of identitarian practice resulted in a narrative where even freed blacks, traveling across country to form new townships after the Civil War, would find themselves utilizing their own inventions of color-coded standards of community membership that were absolutely related to the systems of color and status that had been practiced on them since the days of slavery. You do what you know.

In Johnson's *Middle Passage*, the belly of the ship carries stolen property (in the form of a shape-changing Allmuseri god) that, despite its clear origin, seemed as available to claim as property, even as it competed for attention and protection with the treasures stored near the captain's quarters — merchandise (like men) that was stolen from the various civilizations the ship had contacted.

His biggest crates of plunder from every culture conceivable . . . were wrenched open, spilling onto the sloping floor bird-shaped Etruscan vases, Persian silk prayer carpets, and portfolios of Japanese paintings on rice paper. Temple scrolls I found, precious tablets, and works so exotic to my eyes that Falcon's crew of fortune hunters could have taken them only by midnight raids and murder. Slowly, it came to me, like the sound of a stone plunked into a pond, that he had a standing order from his financiers, powerful families in New Orleans who underwrote the *Republic*, to stock Yankee museums and their homes with whatever of value was not nailed down in the nations he visited. To bring back slaves, yes, but to salvage the best of their war-shocked cultures too. (Johnson 1998, 48–49)

That illegally gained booty and that property contest the very notion of alienability that gives the story its most consistent contours. To whom do the spoils of war and slavery belong? Whether Isabella who marries Rutherford belongs to him or to Zerengue, the man who financed the voyage, or whether the captain's stolen goods were worth the perverse and malignant practices of enslavement for men who became his property during his voyage, or whether the spiritual being at the bottom of the ship had the final say is the novel's compelling interrogative. Whatever its problem, it is, from the story's opening paragraphs to the last, a narrative engagement of how Rutherford "would feel that freedom was property. Power was property. Love of race and kin was property, and if the capital in question was the lives of other colored men . . . well, mightn't a few have to perish, in the progress of the race, for the good of the many?" (ibid., 199).

Imagined Liberalism

It is certainly true that a fiction is an imagined narrative. But fiction is also the space where practical substance is imaginatively engaged. One way to consider the evolution and identity of the nation's literature is to wonder how our fictions could do anything other than reflect the boundedness by law that structured colonial, postcolonial, and even contemporary social and political relations. If law and the customs of property have an inevitable intersection, how could fictive literatures—those that Samuel Taylor Coleridge claimed have an origin in a mechanical fancy and ultimately re-create and or repeat our natural world in order to reach the imaginative—avoid replicating the facts that were so rigorously constructed that they were constitutionally enshrined?[18] The answer is that they did not. Fiction's liberal imagination intersects with the facts of their juridical generation and intimacies.

Perhaps inadvertently, but nonetheless decidedly, thematic consistencies in African American literature in U.S. literatures helped to instantiate the legal fiction of African American persons. The subjects of fiction, especially when composed by black writers who were themselves avatars of the society that created them, seemed unable or unwilling to detach from the regulatory environs in which their authors lived and wrote, and found their own identities subject to the conjunction between race and voice like Countee Cullen's sad notice of his own racial captivity: "To make a poet black *and* bid him sing."[19] African American fiction inevitably reproduced the fictions of their own constitution. The creative potential resident in these associations were too rich a terrain to avoid. In fact, they may even have been aspirational.

From the mid-1800s to the early years of the twentieth century, black writers followed the textual complications of characters whose lives and yearnings entwined with their legal status. In *Clotel; or, The President's Daughter* (1853) William Wells Brown signaled the alterity of its title character with the conjunction—"or"—that ties the book's two titles together.[20] She is both a woman named Clotel *as well as* the daughter of an enslaved woman and Thomas Jefferson, the man who would be president of the United States. The story line extends from that complication of public and private identities. Little wonder that Harriet Jacobs's *Incidents in the Life of a Slave Girl* (1861) found similar resonance in a story of captivity and danger, writing of a woman whose bodily freedom was compromised by the white man who, according to the laws of the era, correctly understood that she was his property, and that his value and conduct toward her and her enslaved children would properly extend from that presumptive and legally inscribed status.[21] The conflated center of *Incidents* literally shapes the enslaved woman's refuge from the threat of sexual violence. The Jacobs chapter most frequently referenced in African American letters, "The Loophole of Retreat," reveals an attic as the hiding place where Linda Brent finds a restricted refuge and a space to secretly watch her children. It is a physically confining space but necessary to avoid the threat of death from her master (Dr. Flint). She endures the confines of an attic imprisonment for seven years, a pitiful synthesis of domesticity and property. It is not the only place in the novel where property and violence are twinned. Dr. Flint threatens to imprison her in a cabin in the woods where he can use his property as he pleases. The common law notion of property that emerged from Roman law's concept of *dominium* and that codified the essential philosophy that property would mean both the right to use and abuse (or consume) a thing, within the limits of the law—*ius utendi et abutendi re sua, quatenus iuris ration patitur*.[22] Her brother and children are imprisoned when she runs away. Brent first takes refuge under the floorboards of her white benefactress's home. As in Morrison's *Beloved*, the regulatory authority of the Fugitive Slave Act controls the narrative. It leaves Brent a prisoner in her employer's home because she knows she can and will be returned to slavery if she is discovered. The attic "loophole of retreat" is only a sanctuary of her mind, certainly not in the bodily constrictions and physical pains that accompany her stay there. But its site as domestic refuge where the property of her body becomes her own only through this tortuous imprisonment underscores the complex and differential effects of a claim to property.

At the turn of the century, Charles Chesnutt's *The Marrow of Tradition* (1901) reversed the perspective but not the subject and took *un*lawfulness as its text. The novel's focus was a factual narrative that had at its center the 1898 Wilmington, North Carolina, race riots, a revolution fomented by the volatile mix of color, class, and the developing political power of postreconstruction blacks that threatened the value and heritage of white privilege. The rebellion that forms the core of the novel is triggered by the sense of political violation and color-coded vulnerability tied to the offending potential that the development of an independent black press and increasingly visible black middle class could exert on white propertied difference.

In *When Whites Riot*, scholar Sheila Smith McKoy calls attention to the crime of rape that formed the narrative core of the riot.[23] Instead of the charges being leveled against black men, McKoy records the origin of the outrage as the moment that the Wilmington black press wrote an editorial naming the crime as one perpetrated against black women "in an attempt to call attention to the number of black women raped by white men who assaulted them *without fear of legal repercussion*" (McKoy 2001, 34, my emphasis). McKoy correctly focuses on the legal frame of this event and included at least implicitly is the constitutional guarantee of freedom of the press — the exercised liberty that earns the black journalists and citizens the violent ire of the white community. In his novel Chesnutt did the same thing when, using a constitutionally framed enumeration of wrongs, he explains the background that led to the rebellion, historically documented in the Wilmington riot of 1898:

> The petty annoyances which the whites had felt at the spectacle of a few negroes in office; the not unnatural resentment of a proud people at what had seemed to them a presumptuous *freedom of speech* and lack of deference on the part of their inferiors, — these things, which he knew were to be made the excuse for overturning the city government, he realized full well were no sort of justification for the wholesale murder or other horrors which might well ensue before the day was done. (Chesnutt 1901, 291, my emphasis)

The crux of Chesnutt's novel is the lawlessness of the rebellion as well as the inability to imagine (a literally constrained imagination) the black woman as a potential victim of a crime. Chesnutt intentionally complicates the utility of the juridical by pointing out the purpose of law's reliable structuring of social order despite the fact that legal redress is obviously alienated when laws are mediated by color. Even at this edge of the twentieth century, black literature, race, and law were inextricably intertwined and creatively provocative.

Just a bit past a decade into the twentieth century, when James Weldon Johnson wrote his fictional *Autobiography of an Ex-Colored Man* (1912), the creative potential in a story line that problematized color and identity and the legal frame that bound the two was evident. Johnson's narrative is suffused with the differences that race makes. There seems to be no home place for this narrator. His travels take him across the world but the discussions he has with fellow travelers nearly always returned to the "Negro question." Almost as if it were carried along with him, like property (like the Invisible Man's briefcase), his status as a Negro was an omnipresent concern; it did not matter where he traveled—in Europe or the United States. The issue was consistently articulated through a legal construction. The advice of a white benefactor who tells the narrator to face the fact of the inequity and try to escape the history of laws that established the claims of race as legally bound:

> We hit slavery through a great civil war. Did we destroy it? No, we only changed it into hatred between sections of the country: in the South, into political corruption and chicanery, the degradation of the blacks through peonage, unjust laws, unfair and cruel treatment; and the degradation of the whites by their resorting to these practices; the paralyzation of the public conscience, and the ever overhanging dread of what the future may bring.[24]

The peripatetic wandering of Johnson's narrator, always, it seems, in search of a home and some physical or psychic property he might claim, is indicative of the dislocations of an identity first and finally navigated through color. His travels in Europe and in cities in the North and South of the United States do nothing to separate him from the Negro question. At the performance of Faust in Paris's L'Opera he is at first enchanted and then despairing when he realizes the identity of the "ethereal" young girl seated near to him, who "spoke in low tones in English" to the gentleman who accompanied her. Before the reader fully considers the narrative twist that seems to be in play—that the gentleman and young girl are romantically involved—it turns out that the two are his father and his sister. It is a particularly interesting (albeit credibly strained) shift because both the potential scenario and the actual one make legitimacy the issue.

Johnson takes full creative advantage of the complications that masking color might bring: from a sister who at first appears to be a potential romantic conquest—risking that great taboo of sexually intimate kinship—to pointing out that the anonymous landscape of a Paris opera *house* might bring this family, or at least the father, son, and daughter, home again in ways that U.S. cultures would neither permit nor imagine. They are seated in the most austere cultural hierarchy but also in a domestically attired site with drapes and velvet curtains. Despite the ways in which the intimacy of the encounter teases this domesticity, it is not their home. Surely this high-culture location of their meeting is an intentional statement of irony—a signifying Faustian bargain.

Alongside this critique of hierarchy and paternity, Johnson makes it apparent that the complications of his legal identity follow him whether he travels the old world cities on the European continent or passes through the new democracies of the United States. His color is inescapable, or at least the fact of his preoccupation with its boundaries that follow him even outside of the jurisdictions of U.S. laws. It indicates the psychic state of legal status as his coloring taints every experience that matters enough to capture in this fictive autobiography and to render its title *An Ex-Colored Man* superbly ironic. His home is most reliably a matter of skin and sensibility rather than location. And even though his skin is light enough to pass for white, which the "ex-colored man" eventually does, the book's final lines betray the psychic costs of his transformation into a white man:

> I feel small and selfish. I am an ordinarily successful white man who has made a little money. There are men who are making history and a race. I, too, might have taken part in a work so glorious. . . . When I some-

times open a little box in which I still keep my fast yellowing manu-
scripts, the only tangible remnants of a vanished dream, a dead ambi-
tion, a sacrificed talent, I cannot repress the thought, that, after all, I
have chosen the lesser part, that I have sold my birthright for a mess of
pottage. (Johnson 1912, 93)

A "mess of pottage" is something of little value. It is an ironic comple-
ment to the idea of value that Harris claims in her essay. Nevertheless, the
fact that his whiteness has at least this comparative association illustrates
how the claim of Harris's essay has found a fictive residency as well as a
legal one—the foundational principle of a liberal imaginary. Liberation
as a conceptual principle of the new nation is invested with an originary
contradiction. It incorporates both the liberal subject, one free to constitute both himself and the new nation-state as beholden to the principle of liberalism, as well as a subject whose judgment about liberation
is a self-constructed fiction. A modern liberal personhood was as socially
constrained as the classical claim. Both depended mightily on who had
the social standing to articulate a private personhood that would sustain
its coherence in public. As I argue elsewhere, that kind of person is privileged by a complementary status that is socially normative: white, heterosexual, and male.[25] The fictions of enslavement, whether written during or
close to the era, or as neo–slave narratives, perhaps seem too convenient
to illustrate this claim of an inherently compromised principle of a person
as property as intrinsic to African American letters. Novels written at the
end of the twentieth century and into the twenty-first are similarly pre-
occupied and give additional credence to this theory of property.

Mapping Racial Reason

"They shoot the white girl first." Toni Morrison wrote in the first line of
her 1998 novel *Paradise*.[26] "With the rest" the novel's second line explains,
"they can take their time." These two statements constitute as bold and
intriguing an opening as exists in U.S. literatures and instantiate the com-

plex readings that will be the novel's abiding accompaniment. One reading might engage the racialisms that underlie the novel's declarative opening. Another reveals the contingencies implicit in the tangle of race and identity. "They can" — as in *they are able to* — "take their time." What is it about the "rest" that allows them this comparative laxity? Anticipation of the reader's well-socialized judgment here is key — they must not be white. And at the opening of the novel, it also seems that this distinction must have some meaning, some critical resonance to the story that unfolds.

Morrison's craft is fully on display here. Depending greatly on a readership for whom race matters, Morrison crafts a narrative that subverts that material difference and creates hierarchies of class, color, sexualities, and gender that are interpretively significant at the same moment that she disemploys race as a significant difference. The only way race can matter is if a reader searches the story for the one girl who is white. However, critical and more skillful readers will allow the narrative to overtake their initial interrogative interests in sussing out and assigning racial categories to the women. If this happens, a rich and provocative story emerges that is certainly riveted to identities and the regulations that relationships and communities impose but it does not depend on a lawyerly discovery process. This narrative emerges on its own without the impulsive oversight of a readership inclined to discern racial identities that inevitably exert their own interpretive biases.

This boundedness of a reader's expectation and textual result does not escape the narrative juridical engagement. They are relocated to two properties — a piece of land named Haven and a former gambler's mansion/schoolhouse/convent where a series of abandoned women come to seek sanctuary. It is worth noting here how frequently fiction encourages the religious codes' collision with the legal. It's as if that early Virginia declaration of which persons might anticipate freedom (Christians) that was eventually discarded and replaced with black folk never disinvested from the imaginative potential of that choice between religion or race as identities that mattered. The pairing is not unreasonable. Law and religion are both regulatory systems that compete for control over the body politic and oftentimes clash in their authoritative claims.

In *Paradise*, black families who leave Minnesota and trek across the country do so in order to escape the laws of race that would determine their social standing. So the narrative about a migrant community is at first situated in laws that notice that dislocated community's racial identity. Morrison turns this hierarchy into the self-imposed hierarchies of color—light skinned black folk and dark 8-rock (coal black) ones. But even these differences depend on knowing and replicating the social imposition of superficial distinctions that make little sense even as they impose substantial differences in potential and even freedom. "I did that on purpose," Morrison explains. "I wanted the readers to wonder about the race of those girls until those readers understood that their race didn't matter. I want to dissuade people from reading literature in that way." She adds: "Race is the least reliable information you can have about someone. It's real information, but it tells you next to nothing."[27]

Morrison could only engage race in order to disengage it in a literary and social culture that had grown to understand and read according to the ways in which race mattered. In order to dispose of unreliable but fully socialized habits, Morrison had to at first notice them in order to effectively render them impotent.

In *Paradise*, a novel that offers many lenses into what a sanctuary might be like if race lost its force, Morrison indicates the way in which some other form of instantiated difference—colorism, gender, family—will displace that effective distinction of race. The omnipresent question that saturates the story is whether there is a sanctuary in paradise? And even though race does not matter in ways that shape character and identity in this novel, race matters as an *expectational* structure of reading ("They shoot the white girl first") and an *aspirational* structure of her writing— a narrative with a goodly amount of "real information," but information that ultimately "tells you next to nothing." Even though the shape of her story makes certain this is true, race was, nevertheless, the generative architecture of identity from which everything else—social laws, customs, habits, and laxities—take their cue even when the cue is to displace one for the other.

The women who took refuge in the former convent took refuge there to escape the tragedies of their lives. They were fugitives living in a liminal space outside of a community that had made their own fugitivity their controlling regulation. The group of men from the nearby town of Haven (later renamed Ruby by its inhabitants) descended on the house of outcasts to wipe out the chaotic contamination that the women living there brought to their town. Of course, the novel reveals that the men's rule-bounded habits are the source of their own problems. But Morrison's suture of their fixation with order and the laws of identity follows a map of racial reasoning that traces the now familiar route in black novels of recalling persons as property.

The men of Ruby were descended from a generation of midnight-skinned black folk who founded a town they named "Haven" in the late 1800s. Their journey away from the sites of slavery where their bodies were property (whether during the era of slavery itself or in the neo-enslavement of the southern sharecropping system) into the expanse of the American West where they might locate a property *outside of themselves* to own and order was complicated when they found themselves "disallowed" by towns established by light-skinned ex-slaves and freedmen. In response to this rejection, the founders of Haven, patriarchs of nine families with notably dark ("8-rock"—the "deep-deep" level in a coal mine) coloring, developed a set of principles for governance that would elevate their pure-black line of descendency worthy of protection. Their blackness became a property for conversion. Their progeny are directed to marry dark-skinned women and rejected when they attempt to bring a light-skinned black into their family. It's a blood-borne value formed in direct opposition to the normative white and lightness that slavery and its aftermath elevated. In other words, and in order to spite their histories, they practiced property conversion—notably an unlawful act, a taking of someone else's property—when they turned their dark bodies into a value for themselves, rather than for white owners. But it was also a value that instantiated an effective rule of law, or code of conduct, that was modeled after the only one they knew well enough and intimately enough to reject through an apposite structure. These founding fathers were as bound by law as the nation they escaped from, and they were as attached to the idea of order through law in order to form the nation whose ideals would lend a particularly raced contour to their navigations.

Ruby was the second iteration of Haven, the town borne of a "Disallowing." It was (re)built in the 1940s, keeping intact (rebuilding) at its center the only physical reminder of the first settlement, a large brick oven with words carved into its façade that seemed designed to govern the town's judgments and conduct—except that they were an enigma. The words might have read, "be the furrow of his brow" or "beware the furrow of his brow." In a provocative rendering of constitutional interpretational schemes, no one is able to recall the original language or discern its original intent. So the wording became as open and vulnerable to interpretation as the town was to the vices that resulted from its self-imposed isolation and its stubborn governance by whoever was a true-blood descendant of the dark-skinned founding families: "'Beware the Furrow of His Brow?' 'Be the Furrow of His Brow?' Her own opinion was that 'Furrow of His Brow' alone was enough for any age or generation. Specifying it, particularizing it, nailing its meaning down, was futile. The only nailing needing to be done had already taken place. On the Cross. Wasn't that so?" (93).

The story cannot escape the racialized constitution that governs it. With the glimmer of religious reasoning as an imagined body ("the only nailing needing to be done had already taken place. On the Cross"), their need escaped that boundedness and attached to social determination that was religiously enforced. And it was a question of property. Whoever owned the legacy of the oven stood to be as important a figure as the interpretive "constitutional" authority. So the townsfolk relinquished themselves to it in a rite as religious as it was regulatory when they forced their racial identity into a way of determining their place in society. Whether this particular story's telling is the imagination of a twentieth-century writer reconstituting the lives of black folk who lived a full century before she was even born, or the imaginative lives of those characters played out in the story, a social contract that embeds the notion of people as real estate regulates the outcome. Morrison made this conflict a part of her craft, recognizing the competing systems that could hold the story's telling in its grasp but trying first "to enunciate and then eclipse the racial gaze altogether." In "Home," Morrison continues:

> I want to inhabit, walk around, a site clear of racist detritus; a place where race both matters and is rendered impotent. . . . The overween-ing, defining event of the modern world is the mass movement of raced populations. . . . The contemporary world's work has become policing, halting, forming policy regarding and trying to administer the move-ment of people. Nationhood—the very definition of citizenship—is constantly being demarcated and redemarcated in response to exiles, refugees, *Gastarbeiter*, immigrants, migrations, the displaced, the flee-ing, and the besieged. The anxiety of belonging is entombed within the central metaphors in the discourse . . . the fictions of sovereignty. Yet these figurations of nationhood and identity are frequently as raced themselves as the originating racial house that defined them. When they are not raced, they are . . . imaginary landscape, never inscape; Utopia, never home.[28]

The two major residences were themselves competitive: a man-made town and a convent, refurbished for worship but fighting its history (it was built as a brothel) and its current inhabitants (a motley group of for-saken women).

The convent was seventeen miles outside of the town but not far enough away for its contemporary unruliness to threaten the governance of Ruby. In stark contradiction to the town, there are no rules, and there was no color-coding in the Convent. What happens to them is a conse-quential invasion of custom and regulation—a violent way of seeing and the consequential violence of conduct that accompanies it. The men of

Ruby who bring their violence and violations to the place, as evidenced in the novel's first lines, do so from some set of boundaries that the convent's disorder and sanctuary belie. Despite the differences of place, the competing sites in *Paradise*, Ruby and the convent, both are properties that depend on the persons that inhabit them.

Although their ownership seems to depend on the success of a form of governance, the concentration of complex identities and the ambiguity that Morrison posits at the novel's outset makes this impossible. Whether one was a descendent of the eight-rock families or a wayward and abandoned girl who found sanctuary in the Convent, no system of laws — neither the rigid patriarchy that rules Ruby nor the loose necessity that collects wounded women in the convent — survives the grip of social identities. Neither can it codify the brutality the women have endured. Ruby is a place "where race both matters and is rendered impotent."[29] When the men of Ruby come to destroy the place that in their minds is the cause of their failing authority in their own homes and in the town they build to withstand and speak back to the racisms of the era, they "shoot the white girl first" because race matters and because it is impotent. The boundaries they imposed on their own generations — who might marry whom, how difference between light- and dark-skinned refugees or children mattered — could not be sustained within the boundaries of their property. Although the novel's first line would seem to ask for a narrative response — which is the white girl? Morrison explores the multiple potentials in how something that can both "matter and [be] impotent."

The various locations of the novel do expose ways in which race, color, and identity are vulnerabilities that matter. But the properties themselves — neither the mansion's phallic images that the church destroyed when they turned it into a religious domicile in an emblematic confrontation of religious and secular patriarchies, nor the town's failure to find an efficient and useable set of rules — struggle with the composition of their identities. But it's the structure rather than the substance that mattered — how the identitarian focus and the terror that were artificially attached to these properties—the town, the convent, and the women who resided in both ultimately disabled the inhabitants. All were subjected to a patriarchal violence that sutured the outcome of race and rights.

The crew of outraged men determined to bring some familiar and familial-based order back to their town are deputized to take down the out-of-bounds living happening in the house outside of the town's borders. And the very first thing they do is to shoot a white girl and shift the focus of a narrative about property into a something that masks as a mystery about identity. Otherwise, the story's telling could be a travelogue, a journey marked by the intersections of color and place and character. Before race intervened, *Paradise* traced desire. The women who took refuge in the one-time convent occupy the haven they sought rather than the identities the reader struggles to discern. It could have been a novel with illustrative cartography as scaffolding, a map that marked a journey from southern to northern hemispheres, from slave states to free and from free states to "wild" western frontiers. But because the townsfolk had regulated themselves into a population concerned more with rules, legacy, ritual, and their constitution by affiliations or disaffiliations, the reader knows, even without being told, that these men who bring a gun into the convent are people of color. But of course, that is the easily familiar and alternative reading of Morrison's novel. It is cognizable in the same way that Morrison could reasonably anticipate her readers' desire to recognize which one of the residents was the white girl.

The escaped and freed slaves left the South and traveled west looking for a land that would hold them without hostility. During their travels, almost every deed done was encapsulated in some form of structured regulation that proved the uniquely American evolution of their identity. The rules always mattered and constitute their conduct. The dark-skinned paternal rule of the eight-rock families separated themselves into a tribal affiliation marked by color shifting the ways in which their color barred them from settling in other towns where escaped, or newly freed persons of African descent found sanctuary. Indeed they configured a way to make the property of their unadulterated blackness a value. And by giving a legal standing to the ways in which they regulated whom their children could marry, using the same constructedness as the southern society they had left, they built a social hierarchy that designated them as the families with the most power.

The cultural construct of racial passing, consistent with the propertied notion of "trespass" when it came to the bodies of enslaved Americans, followed them out of slavery and continued its regulatory hold in the scores of years that followed. Clubs were formed that depended on blue-veined lightness, paper-bag coded color and hair that could not entrap a writing tool. And in Morrison's *Paradise*, a town was formed that privileged playing in the dark. They could no more escape the appeal of legal constitution than they could the consequences of the felt-life of color-coded conduct. They formed policies about color and class with as much ease and determination as they managed the moves necessitated by their lock-step focus on legislated identity. They even gave it the ritual trappings of a legal framework. Their ceremonial undoing of the by-now brittle bricks of the oven from one town's center to another as if its cindered interiors or brittle words could reform the governing regulation that once identified the town's center and its meaning was precedent on the move. Ownership of the thing, which would include determining the meaning of its faded constitution, was the desiderata.

Being in Place: Landscape, Never Inscape

Paradise has its entailments—it is propertied, owned, and alienable. All are consistent with a literary tradition that is persistently encumbered with the consequences of ownership and the complexities inherent to the vexed ontologies attached to U.S. formations of property.

Whether they are contemporary narratives like Octavia Butler's *Kindred*,[30] written in the tradition of the neo–slave narrative that pulls her character back in time to days in which she became enslaved and someone's property, or Johnson's *Middle Passage* that reenacts the liminal in-between of being, owning, and governance, the degree that they are bound by law configures the stuff and substance of black fictions.

Herein lies the conundrum. Is property an alienable thing that follows its Justinian origins of use and abuse? Or is property the thing you are—inalienable, and despite or in fact precisely *because* of the penumbras of legal histories that attempted to overwrite the first code of a partial body—always and inevitably attached to the black body it has both parsed and formulated?

Stephen Best's *The Fugitive's Property* critically understands this puzzlement, considering "property's drift in the direction of the commodification of personhood" under the rubric of "property's personification" in a perceptive reading of the complex problematic of the paradox of black ontology.[31] However, an essential question remains that seems to have its origins before the "drift" that Best takes as his starting place. This contingent intimacy that produces a legal fiction is what assures and produces the narrative complexities that so preoccupy the literature of black America. When the ethic of use and abuse attached to persons who were property became constitutive, how, then, did blacks reconstitute their own bodies within the same law that had dismembered them? Best's perspective is to honor the dismemberment and "drift" toward a theory of voice, one that perversely coheres to "the notion of a person [that] was at once fragmented into its various attributes, capacities and properties" (Best 2004, 38). But the literature of this tradition actually proffers a narrative somewhat different from this. In U.S. black literatures' preoccupation with coherence and embodied "properties," "appropriations," "proprietary rights," and even with what is "appropriate" one sees the trace of the racial body.

The examples nearly overwhelm. They are evident in how, in Ntozake Shange's *For Colored Girls*, "bein alive & bein a woman & bein colored is a metaphysical dilemma / I havent conquered yet"; and in the way in which the critical question for Toni Cade Bambara's Velma in *The Salt Eaters* is "Are you sure, sweetheart, that you want to be well" (3)? Minnie Ransom, a healer, warns Velma that "wholeness is no trifling matter" (10).³² Are Shange's women or Morrison's in *Paradise*, or Bambara's Minnie ready to take ownership of themselves? In fact, in these literatures that explore illness and displacement, the central question is the location of the self. What property might it claim when the race that would name it could also diminish the value of or within the claim?

This locative interplay is critical to Melvin Dixon's *Vanishing Rooms* where one of the characters is actually named "Rooms," and the novel depends on a series of boardinghouses, homes, and warehouses to stand in for places that should be safe.³³ Dixon's novel depends on a constructed but vulnerable lacunae between location and ontology:

> "You have good family waiting for you. You have Rooms. You'll be all right."
>
> "Rooms? I don't need no boardinghouse," Phillip said. He started looking past Jesse and me like he was trying to see the outside. Beyond the visitors' door, that is.
>
> "I mean Rooms," Jesse said, pointing to me. "She'll take good care of you."
>
> "That's what he calls you?" Phillip asked. He looked disturbed.
>
> My silence answered for me.
>
> "I don't like that. You're not a place, Shit, you're a person." (Dixon 1991, 138–139)

In fact, it is the ontological ease of this question from the *materia* of (a) body to sites outside of it—what might (be a) place for a visitor and what might be (a) home—that marks this literature's residue of legal property. In "Home" Morrison notes the importance of "not only the safety and freedom . . . but . . . contemporary searches and yearnings for social space that is psychically and physically safe" (10). It's a challenge U.S. black literatures consistently engage.

In Paule Marshall's *Brown Girl, Brownstones* Silla's father Deighton is taunted for not having "buy house" in the United States—the piece of property he owns in Barbados is unrecognizable as a commitment to the new homeland. Vanessa Dickerson argues for the ontological substance of these property matters in her perceptive essay, "A Property of Being" about Marshall's novel.[34] As Dickerson has noticed, *Brown Girl's* legalisms regarding property not only determine character—is Deighton a "buy house" immigrant?—but they dictate act, location, and consequence (1991). Deighton's wife Silla forges his signature in order to get the property she covets, and as a consequence of Silla's testimony, her husband is deported as an illegal alien. Deighton dies before he gets back to his homeland. Silla is left stateside with her illegally gotten gain (a brownstone) and a guilt-ridden grief over the loss of her husband. In *Stigmata*, Phyllis Alesia Perry's character Lizzie begins to manifest stigmata-like wounds that appear to be most like slave manacles even though Lizzie lives in an era more than a century removed from slavery.[35] Items from a trunk (an inherited item like Rutherford's portmanteau and the briefcase that was a gift to Ellison's Invisible Man) slip Lizzie into days where either mental illness or a memory of slavery sends her to a mental asylum. The effort toward coherence (even as it suffers the potential of fragmentation like the consequence literally felt by Butler's Dana) of black fiction in the United States is a direct address to the ontological puzzlement of the body being its own attribute while maintaining the situational ethic of prevailing legalisms as the thing that threatens fracture. In Morrison's *Sula*, property, value, and being constitute Sula's penultimate reflection regarding her friendship with Nel. Sula understands Nel's loss is in her having placed a value on their friendship; while Sula had always thought that what belonged to one girl belonged to the other, because their inseparability as friends meant their inseparability as bodies. "She will walk on down that road, her back so straight . . . thinking how much I have cost her and never remember the days when we were two throats and one eye and we had no price" (147). Or, from the perspective of *Paradise*, if we can only put the oven back together again, we might have the original words—and recover their intent. This yearning is, as the men in *Paradise* discover, a project in futility—landscape, never inscape.

Although "three-fifths" is a fraction made whole with full personhood and citizenship, citizenship does not endow one with a completed humanity. Citizenship is the way in which the law recognizes—or does not recognize—persons. And it does so with a peculiarity of language that points to the origins of our considerations that divided humans into different classes by race. A "naturalized" citizen is constitutionally recognized in Article 1, which calls for a "uniform" Rule of Naturalization. In the years immediately following the Constitution's ratification, the language of naturalization ("any alien, being a free white person who shall have resided within the limits and under the jurisdiction of the United States for a term of two years") was absolutely attached to the principle that mattered to the nation.[36] Whiteness was the single value to be legally inscribed and constitutionally protected. Ian Lopez makes the association plain: "In every naturalization act from 1790 until 1952, Congress included the 'white person' prerequisite" and "opted to maintain the prerequisite" even when naturalization was extended to blacks, or "persons of African nativity, or African descent."[37] In other words, even as U.S. policies eased and allowed others into the rights of the nation, it was by extension of the privilege of whiteness (at the end of World War II explicitly naming races indigenous to North and South America, Filipinos and Chinese) rather than a revision of the white persons prerequisite—the identity that historically leads as text in these immigration reformulations.

In fact, the use of the word *naturalized* and the vocabularies produced in immigration issues—"aliens, undocumented, and illegals"—are a direct consequence of the prerequisite clause that continues, even in the twenty-first century, to govern the nation's perception of citizenship and perception of those who would enter the United States and claim what are ultimately the values descended from whiteness. These vocabularies continue to attach to bodies that yearn for legal (rather than fugitive) cognizance within the law. The assurance of some form of fugitivity populating the black text is the conundrum that matters as well as structures this literature's investment in the law. If law can make a man, it can unmake them. Not unlike a critically ungendered (but fully sexualized) reading of Frederick Douglass's struggle with his slave master Covey, legal boundedness is always a storied and contestatory struggle with the potential of the fully human. The property might escape, become fugitive, or become legal, but the interrogative of its identity and belongingness—some persistent iteration of the interrogative "whose man are you?"—is an omnipresent and propertied reality, bound by law.

TWO

Bodies as Evidence

(of Things Not Seen)

> A courtroom is a visceral Roman circus. No one involved in this
> contest is, or can be, impartial. . . . For to suspend judgment de-
> mands that one dismiss one's perceptions at the very same moment
> that one is most crucially—and cruelly—dependent on them. . . .
> Our ability to perceive is at once tyrannized by our expectations,
> and at war with them. The light is always changing.
>
> — James Baldwin, *The Evidence of Things Not Seen*

Baldwin's metaphor of the courtroom as circus depends on both the spectacle of the event as well as its competing ambiguities. It operates in a site
designed to highlight the ringmaster as a necessary actor who coordinates
disparate actions. There is a fact finder, and the fabric of facts is complex
and contradictory. That disputatious terrain is where black bodies expose
the legacy of legal difference. They disrupt the coherence of a body politic
that would claim as common the bond of citizenship, and they contradict
and consistently invigorate the national claim of equality under the law.
Little wonder that black bodies, when they enter our national fictions,
serve to confound, contradict, and even instantiate a perverse legibility
that tells the incoherent narrative of America's legal histories of racial
reasoning. The evidence of U.S. blackness stipulates race as a persistent
legalism.

Laws of evidence regulate testimony—which may come in the form of speech or documentary records. Law in the United States followed the history of British common law in using evidence to determine whether information has probative rather than prejudicial values. Judicial frames encourage probity and discourage prejudice and for that reason evidence law emerged alongside a substantial framework of regulations that would govern admissibility. The goal is to mediate fact finding so that a replicable legal process might discover the truth of the matter in question rather than simply compile competing and/or prejudicial narratives that would add to the confusion of an event's potentially multifaceted explication. The courtroom performs as if it is not Baldwin's circus. It arranges for experts and lay persons—reasonable persons in the parlance of the law— to contribute to establishing evidence as witnesses. A judge and/or jury stand as finders of fact, sorting through the narratives and legal claims to reach resolution.

In literature, readers serve the adjudicative role, sifting between various narratives, sometimes improbable, incomplete, and at other times fully incredible in order to determine the narrative facts that fictions compose. Notably, in fiction, the potential of plural truths is preserved and is often even the objective. In that process, racial complexity is a fixed apparition.

Given is a history of laws and practices of literature that embody the very bodies (black and colored folk) that complicate a principle of legal neutrality (justice as a blind goddess). In the context of U.S. literatures, evidence might be best understood as the thread that links a claim to its outcome. Because race matters in the United States, because it is woven into the fabric of citizenship, idolatry, and privilege, the thread is embodied.

Consider these two cases that reached the U.S. Supreme Court. Both involved the kind of maritime misadventures that became the stuff of Johnson's fiction of the *Middle Passage*. Each turns on questions of property and evidence that are both literally and figuratively exchangeable. The *Antelope* and the *Amistad* were slave ships. Although their cargo was human, some of that cargo was adjudicated as property, and some were held to be legal persons. There was no visible difference that would make the distinction. All were black men, women, and children from West Africa destined to slavery in the Americas.[1]

The ship that left Baltimore in 1819 was registered under Venezuelan identity as the *Columbia*. It sailed to Africa's west coast and pirated ships there, including the American registered ship the *Exchange* (later renamed the *Arraganta*). In the course of its attacks, it captured a Spanish ship, the *Antelope*, and took over its cargo of over one hundred and fifty West Africans destined for enslavement. Following the well-worn routes of the triangle slave trade, both ships—the *Arraganta* and the *Antelope*—headed for Brazil where the *Arraganta* capsized. That ship's cargo—including the West Africans—was then transferred to the *Antelope* and the *Antelope* proceeded by itself to complete the triangle route, heading north to reach the eastern coast of the United States. By that time there were nearly three hundred West Africans in manacles being readied for sale in Florida. However, before the disembarkation and sale could proceed, a United States revenue cutter arrested the process and led the ship to Savannah. In a hot Savannah courtroom three nations—Spain, Portugal, and the United States—lay claim to the human cargo.[2] Circuit Court Justice William Johnson heard the case and eventually ruled that the enslaved would be "apportioned by lottery among American, Spanish, and Portuguese claimants."[3]

On appeal to the Supreme Court, Chief Justice Marshall, author of the court's opinion, noted the competing interests of the claimants: "These Africans . . . insist on their right to freedom and submit their claim to the laws of the lands, and to the tribunals of the nation. The Consuls of Spain and Portugal, respectively, demand these Africans as slaves, who have, in the regular course of legitimate commerce, been acquired as property by the subjects of their respective sovereigns, and claim their restitution under the laws of the United States."[4]

The legal question in this matter rested on whether the physical evidence was property to be restituted or persons to be freed. In an arguably Solomon-like decision (absent its moral authority), Justice Marshall divided the *materia*. Some were judged to be property and returned to Spain to be treated as such under Spanish law. But the overwhelming majority was determined to have originated from the U.S. ship (the *Antelope*). Since the United States had outlawed the importation of slaves trade in 1808 any commercial transaction was illegal. Because of the court's ruling, these Africans became persons entitled to freedom and were subsequently repatriated to West Africa, to the country now known as Liberia. During the presentation of the case, Justice Marshall required some evidentiary proof of ownership from the countries that claimed them. Of the foreign nations involved, only Spain was able to make a credible proffer.

The confusions of names in this case, the various ports of embarkation and attempted disembarkation, the capsizing and shifts of the "cargo" from one vessel to the other seem emblematic of a legacy of confusion that followed a law that could hold, given the correct proffer, that people were property. But ironically, property could not *give* evidence—they could only *be* evidence. Certainly such an entanglement has the potential makings of existential fiction.

The *Amistad* case, argued nearly two decades later, is a more familiar history to U.S. readers. There was a rebellion aboard the slave ship *Amistad* after it left Cuba in 1839. As a consequence of the battle, the ship changed hands from Cuban slavers to its Mende captives. The West Africans demanded the ship sail toward their homeland, but the navigator deceived them and secretly steered toward the U.S. east coast. There the crew from a revenue cutter, like the one that had previously stopped the *Antelope*, managed to secure it from the Mende rebels. The Africans were turned over as captives to the U.S. government, and the claims to them began with the issue of identity. What were these captives? The Spaniards called for the surrender of the insurrectionists and named them as murderers (which would make them persons), rather than property. They based their claim on the treaty that declared maritime slave trading illegal. If they were going to Spanish hands, their identity had to be legally cognizable. However, given maritime regulations regarding the slave trade, the captives could not legally be property. It was an exquisitely turned argument. Former president John Quincy Adams argued a portion of the case on the behalf of New England abolitionists and claimed that the massacre committed by the Mende was the natural consequence of a reasonable desire for freedom. Adams cites the *Antelope* decision in his argument for the freedom of the captives from the *Amistad*, chiefly to note the libel in the testimony of the Spanish and Portuguese vice counsels in reference to what number of Africans "belonged" to them. Adams declared that case to be

> so extraordinary, so anti-judicial is every thing upon the records in this case of the *Antelope*, that the Supreme Court actually did not know what was the question upon which the judges of the Circuit Court were opposed in their opinion. . . . Evidence was deemed sufficient, which, upon an ordinary question of property . . . would have been rejected as inadmissible. . . . What could the court do? The United States regard the subjects of this suit [the *Amistad*] as men and not things.[5]

The two legal cases have all the makings of a postmodern fiction—characters exchanging places between persons and things, language so convoluted and names so easily dropped and replaced that identity seems a free-floating signifying question with a critical and necessary propensity for shape shifting. This ease centered on the destabilizing discourse of race. The legal history may offer some sense of origin, at least, for the quixotic properties of property as discussed in the previous chapter, but it also offers a generative structure for the confounding exchange between property being persons and property as an evidentiary *materia*.

Secondhand Tales and Hearsay

Since *kinds* of persons have a peculiar U.S. legal history, the fictive embodiment of evidence, that is, the way in which the bodies that carry the narrative also give evidence for the legal entanglement of these fictions, might have been predictable in a literature that, like law, made color a performative difference in the exposition of text.

It's a very likely explanation for the overlap of narratives in David Bradley's *The Chaneysville Incident* when John Washington, a college history professor, attempts to discover the truth of his father's death and must reach back into the very history he teaches in order to discover the narrative truth his practiced research methodologies had missed.[6] His finely practiced methodologies, so dependently authoritative, nonetheless lacked the requisite standing to tell his father's story. The evidence he would proffer came in the form that common law would recognize — the Euro-American historical narratives found in his texts and reference materials. But these sources had enslaved his imagination, wrapping it into the selective authorities of academic license. In this case, imagination does not mean fancifully impossible, instead it means substantively rich. Professor Washington had to learn that the evidence he needed evolved in a separate sphere — one his academic training had taught him to ignore. He had to pay attention to the unique composition, which meant paying attention to its textu(r)al embodiment. In this way a spoken narrative gains an authority that had no ordinary standing in his discipline. It came from a man he would otherwise have ignored had he not been summoned to his deathbed.

The Chaneysville Incident is as close a conflation of the enslaved narrative with a contemporary moment as one often sees in black literatures, although Octavia Butler's *Kindred* (published just two years earlier in 1979) explored a similarly liberated chronology of imaginative distance, as Butler's character Dana travels back and forth between her enslaved past and her present marriage to a white man. Like Bradley's black professor, whose partner Judith is white, Dana's own interracial marriage navigates a complex personal color line. It has to instruct their legal partners who share with them every other intimacy but the unknowable privations of a black identity. In fact, one might argue that exposure to those interracial intimacies enabled some liberation from ordinarily racialized boundaries. These characters could have experienced some degree of exception from a past history of color boundedness, arguably escaping the color line — that is, until Dana went back home. But like Morrison's rememory, and like legal precedent, the past is both present and disruptive.

In Bradley's novel, the evidence that will not dissipate is the narrative told by his father's dying friend. Old Jack summons the professor to his deathbed in order to give a testimonial John could not get from his father or his grandfather—both of whom were dead—or from the historical records his father left in his mother's keeping. In fact the professor had ignored the ledger, thinking it was a bootlegger's record and had no place in his structured, legal research.

The novel's exposition entails all the forms of fiction's improbabilities, and at first the reader is co-opted as well, bound by the finesse of the historian's clearly trained but inevitably shackled thinking. John worries that "there had been too many stories, told over too many years . . . they all blurred together in my mind. And then I began to think about what a man's dying really means: his story is lost. Bits and pieces of it remain, but they are all *secondhand tales and hearsay*, or cold official records that preserve the facts and spoil the truth" (Bradley 1990, 48). Here, Bradley has it exactly right to direct the reader away from this historian's refined understanding of facticity and look instead to the spoken word testimony for the truth the professor is after. Notably, Bradley casts the fact finding within the frames of the law. The historian is summoned to hear a dying man's testimonial and through that legally bound narrative, the truth will out.

In the laws that govern the admissibility of evidence, dying declarations survive the regulations of inadmissible hearsay. John has already presumptively labeled Jack's story as "secondhand stories and hearsay." Dying testimonials rise above a hearsay challenge based on the legal reasoning that the final words of a dying person are presumed to have no investment in anything other than truth. Although many readers of literature especially might pause at that pregnant opportunity for deceit, the law has reasoned it into admissibility rather than pursued the rich potential of deathbed conceits (and the treatment of false confessions, as another example).

In a convenient illustration of the thesis of this book, that black literatures are legal fictions inevitably bound by law, Bradley represents dying Old Jack's declaration as having a unique veracity amongst the many stories that Professor Washington complains of as clutter. John Washington, who had ignored the man while he pursued his academic research, is folded into the gravity of the moment when the story begins with all the structural architecture of testimony: "I recall the night I met him," he said. "It musta been near fifty year ago now, but I recollect it clear. It was in the back room a Hawley's store. Halfways through a Saturday night" (51). Already Jack's narrative has the shape of testimonial truth, with its straightforward clarity and stark and specific recollection of both scene and time. The frame of this telling would have legal credibility. Old Jack's witness would survive a challenge of admissibility. As Bradley composes this story, or allows John Washington to recall Old Jack's voice, he abandons the historiography that Washington's academic background would ordinarily value as reliable and instead depends on the testimonial voice—the oral history—of a man who tells his remembered truth about the death of thirteen black men who committed suicide in what comes to be known as "the Chaneysville incident." Once the professor accepts this testimonial truth, legally forceful because of the evidentiary exclusion from hearsay inherent in a dying declaration, the historian dramatically discards the pens, pencils, pads and "tools of [his] trade." He burns them, satisfied although perplexed that the declaration had a vitality that his learned and honed methodology could not replicate.

Scholar Kenneth Warren recounts this passage as well in his consideration of *What Was African American Literature* (2011).[7] However, Warren submits to the arguably persuasive romance of the fiction, its interest in "collecting stories and memorializing events in a way that turns them into phenomena we must re-experience in order to understand." Warren's perspective that "this [African American] literature seeks to politicize a melancholy truth about the human condition" (102) acknowledges the tone that specifies the consequences of such a deeply emotional hijack. However, in legal terms, Warren's judgment not only has prejudicial instead of probative value; it opens itself to a narrowly legalistic determination that is quite different from the thick terrain and deep structures of literature. My coordinate theory of reading law and literature into a shared racial text claims both the reasoned and judicially narrow legalism *as well as* the complex and provocative consequence of literature. In my judgment, this makes literature significantly more resonant than a narrow period-bound response to Jim Crowism or Civil Rights or even to the era of enslavement that Warren has determined are reasonable brackets of the tradition. However, the consequence of his determined reading seems to have abandoned the skeletal for the more provocative stuff of blood and guts.

Instead of offering a theory of evidence as a response to the codification of black bodies or as a legal maneuver coordinate with legal procedure and decided on the rational basis of the determination of its value to the narrative, in the complex association of law and literature narrative evidence is sutured to the normative response that bonds the body to its frame. No matter how finely wrought, the melancholic appeal that Warren articulates cannot sustain the tradition's long and vigorous history. But law does not tell a story by itself. A literary tradition — even one Warren's text argues as extinct — does not survive by textual hijack. That maneuver is too discrete for metatheoretical rigor. Instead, a robust and legible methodology suggests that the vitality of African American literary fiction cannot fully rest in the diverse and complex stories of the tradition nor in their extraordinarily poignant social circumstances. Instead, the common architectures of their sources and the composition of the bodies both constitute the treasure of the narrative.

Fiction is neither biography nor sociology. It affirms that cultural context is complicated and not "just the patina etched by history upon a universal unchanging self."[8] Crais and Scully make that notation in their text about Sara Baartman subtitled *A Ghost Story and a Biography*. This is a useful if not unusually paired indication of the interlocative relationship between fiction and fact where "paradoxes and silences give us pause. Ghosts haunt [the] pages" (Crais and Scully 2010, 6).

What's of critical use in the passage that Warren perceptively rescues from Bradley's masterful novel is the structural pattern of memorializing through legal reasoning. The suicide of the Chaneysville thirteen is a tropic fugitive act—a rebellion worthy of rememory. It redeploys the black trope of extralegalism through a rebellion that takes place in a specific context of the collision between the permissible and the illegitimate.

The Chaneysville thirteen are men and women whose mythology refuses to relinquish its evidentiary value. Old Jack is their testimonial resurrection. Professor Washington's habits of academic discipline are tainted and flawed, unable to contain the capacious and incoherent evidence of slavery. He finally realizes this when he burns the note cards that were the standard tools of his academic trade. Notably, this significant moment when he admits Old Jack's oral history as reliable evidence that will allow him to recognize the truth of the matter is not the story's only investment and engagement with the law. A white judge, Lucian Scott, offers a funerary call and response at Old Jack's services that strangely has more congregational power at the black gathering than the one offered by John Washington's mother Yvette. Bradley writes, "And then they did something odd—they dropped away and let him [Judge Scott] carry the solo, as if he were one of them" (Bradley 1990, 228). It's a composition that seems to signal the adjudicatory power invested in Judge Scott's role as the fact-finder. His intervention is a powerful signal of how John might reconsider his methodological allegiances. During Jack's otherwise true-to-ritual funeralizing—and until the judge carries the ceremonial call—the illustrative appeal in the law's survival as well as its testimonial authority over both whites and blacks is invested with full symbolic appeal.

The novel also engages a moment of testamentary transfer in the form of a ledger that John's father wills to him but that is withheld not only because of the conditions of the trust but through the machinations of his mother Yvette. She represents the other side of the black literary binary of religious regulation—thematically linked to Baldwin's oppositional proffer of jails or churches. In fact, his mother's house is cluttered with the debris of church pamphlets, her answer to her two sons' troubled efforts at playing in the white worlds — a gamesmanship their education and talents seem to make available to them. The judge is, of course, far from a neutral adjudicator, and he has political ambitions that implicate an unbecoming judicial activism. But he is also a man of power, a reader of wills, an interpreter of law, someone who can and does redistribute and reclassify property and who relies on the appearance or disappearance of evidence to make his activism possible.

It could be a compelling argument to suggest that any story that involves a plot line inclusive of enslaved Africans, whether written during the era of slavery or as a neo–slave narrative, would necessarily beg for this involvement of the juridical. But we have seen with the histories of the *Antelope* and the *Amistad* that judicial reasoning doesn't necessarily follow predictable patterns. Instead, as clearly illustrated in the racial determination cases referenced earlier, the substance of judicial reasonings varied widely, using ancestry, origin, physiognomy, and social science — in particular anthropology — to ground these determinations. In these property cases, especially as they reached appellate and supreme courts, economics mattered greatly, especially rulings that would favor socioeconomic stability. But this variable intent and outcome make law's formulation to both set and overrule precedent uniquely appropriate for a fiction. What better fictive narrative arrangement than an architecture already designed for shape shifting? This thematic propensity becomes substantive rather than simply an opportunistic moment for composition. In black literature, because law is retained as the foundational structure of black corporeality, the contours of embodiments of the enslaved and newly freed were always available for reconfiguration. African American literature cannot simply function as a mirrored mediation, a reflection of its era. This is especially so because the era's foundations are so vexed. Despite Warren's appealing and perceptive review of these boundaries having some symmetry with the beginning and then the end of Jim Crow, this is not a literature that merely reflects the growing and complex socialities of black life in America. What is, however, extant and fully imagined is the way in which black life in America is intimately related to the persistently vigorous constructedness of that life in the law. As long as law matters, and especially as long as law structures the evolution of identity and rights, this association has an assured longevity. In fact, it is constitutive.

The social evolution that pairs jurisprudence and legal theory to the evidence of the black body has occurred because of the necessity attached to the literary imagination. An obscure and likely unanticipated source might explain the association between the literary imagination and social facticity that becomes so critical to black corporeality and its evidentiary values.

In *Biographia Literaria* nineteenth-century British poet and literary theorist Samuel Taylor Coleridge offers a distinction between the imagination and fancy that seems helpful. Coleridge, with an ideology clearly influenced by Kant, explained the differences between the imagination and fancy by exposing the associative relationship between the two. In reading the following, consider law as fancy and literature as the expressive consequence of (a secondary) imagination.

> The Imagination then I consider either as primary, or secondary. The primary Imagination I hold to be the living power and prime agent of all human perception, and as a repetition in the finite mind of the eternal act of creation in the infinite I AM. The secondary Imagination I consider as an echo of the former . . . it dissolves, diffuses, dissipates, in order to recreate . . . it struggles to idealize and to unify. It is essentially vital, even as all objects (as objects) are essentially fixed. . . . FANCY, on the contrary, has no other counters to play with, but fixities and definites. The fancy is indeed no other than a mode of memory emancipated from the order of time and space; while it is blended with, and modified by that empirical phaenomenon of the will. . . . But equally with the ordinary memory *the Fancy must receive all its materials ready made from the law of association.* (Coleridge 2011, 98, my emphasis)

Fancy becomes the formal version of natural law. Coleridge underscores the relatedness between an imaginative creativity and its original fixity. The task of the imagination requires a stable thing to re-create. As if in response, law labors, particularly in its regulatory formation of rules of evidence, to design that stability. It is a collocation of legalisms that scholar Ian Baucom noticed in *Spectres of the Atlantic*, in which he reminds readers that these legalisms nearly require the intervention of the imagination. Baucom writes that "the boast of evidence, however, is that it limits and constrains the promiscuity of the imagination, weds imagination to a liturgy of facts, records, documented events. If to know is always, in part, to imagine, then evidence demands that imagination bind itself to the empirically demonstrable."[9] And in black literatures, this is precisely what happens.

Evidence forms a legible association between the potential of property and the freedoms of contract, and is also relentlessly postmodern. Gayl Jones's *Corregidora* raises the issue of evidence as the crucial text of literally reproducing the past—using the body as evidence, ultimately as the only surviving proof of a past injustice.[10] Jones's character, blues singer Ursa Corregidora, cannot escape the haunt of her past. Although her music is a vehicle for her spirit's escape from that past, it is nonetheless another version of an imaginative liberalism that is as dangerous as it is liberatory. Music would seem a release—much as the sanctuary of *Paradise*'s convent *seems* an escape—but her music carries the memories of her great-grandmother and grandmother, both of whom were raped by Corregidora, their Portuguese slave master. Her great-grandmother is caught in a brutal reality that would make her progeny also her documentary evidence of the rapes. The warning she gives her granddaughter is rigidly legalized: "*They didn't want to leave no evidence of what they done—so it couldn't be held against them. And I'm leaving evidence. And you got to leave evidence too. And your children got to leave evidence. And when it come time to hold up the evidence, we got to have evidence to hold up. That's why they burned all the papers, so there wouldn't be no evidence to hold up*" (Jones 1986, 14).

In a pitiful version of an enslaved body being the only viable evidence of criminal rape, the novel turns on Ursa's ability to wrest herself free from the cycle of her body having to bear and to be its own evidence. Certainly this is also a story that depends on an enslaved history for a version of its legal tangle and in this way pulls substantially from the genre of the neo–slave narrative; but it is also a postmodern story of a contemporary woman whose freedom depends on her liberation from a bounded imagination. Jones uses the blues as her melancholic mechanism. The novel's typography reveals the postmodern complexities inherent in layered narratives: her memories are textually rendered in italics, a penumbral haunt of a past that inserts itself into her present, but that claims its structural, graphic, and strategic difference from the present. It is certainly rememory, but it does not obliterate the insistent, destabilizing postmodernist haunt.

Even Walter Mosley's fully contemporary novel, *The Last Days of Ptolemy Gray*, that seems urban and focused on a story about a ninety-one-year-old man who suffers from dementia, has a considerable investment in law — particularly evidentiary and contractual foundations of law.[11] The frail and elderly Mr. Gray signs onto an experimental (and nonregulated) clinical trial to restore his mental abilities, just so he can remember enough of his own history, and the promise (in the form of a contract he made with a childhood friend) to exact the justice that the murder of his nephew and the decades-ago lynching of his friend, required. Mosley's novel can be read as dependent on the architecture of contract and centered on the promise that motivated Mr. Gray's donation of his body as an exchange for the memory he has lost. But Mosley's novel is also invested enough in evidentiary claims, hidden gold, conflicting testimonies, and intestate transfers to make it readable under a complex web of property law, evidence, and contract.

Critical to this text's argument regarding the legal boundedness of black literatures is an understanding that law's relationship to literature does not exist as an exclusionary device that polices its content. Instead it renders race vulnerable to a national composition that is always explicitly and sometimes implicitly regulated by law. One need not read Ann Petry's "The Witness" to understand the racial thicket of a black teacher's dilemma — whether or not to report a crime of rape and kidnapping committed by a group of his white male students.[12] The students kidnap their teacher, Dr. Shipley, along with a white girl. Both are taken to a barn where the boys brutally rape her. Then they urge Shipley to take his "turn" with her. He refuses. But the boys are socially and legally strategic. "The girl was lying on the floor, half-naked. . . . She looked as though she were dead. They pushed him toward her saying, 'It's your turn.' He balked, refusing to move. . . . They pushed him closer to the girl and someone grabbed one of his hands and placed it on the girl's thigh, on her breasts" (Petry 1995, 216). Well aware of the instrumentality of his race, they make certain that he is a compromised witness whose evidence, if he were to choose to testify, would be tied to his body as well as the students.' One does not need much of an imagination to conjure a courtroom scene with a prosecutor asking the black southern male, "Did you touch her too?" In a contrapuntal language that reminds the reader of Ellison's confounded Invisible Man, the leader of the gang demands:

> "Put the witness here."
> They stood him against the back wall, facing the wall.
> "He's here and yet he ain't here."
> "Ho-daddy's here — and yet — he ain't here."
> "He's our witness." . . . The girl screamed and then the sound was muffled. (215)

The scene is reminiscent of the ontological nullification in the sermon in Ellison's Invisible Man: "'now black is . . .' the preacher shouted. . . . 'an' black ain't. . . . black will git you . . . an' black won't. It do . . . an' it don't'" (Ellison 1995b, 8, 9).

Later, the teacher understands the very predicament that was the text of Ellison's preacher's sermon. In a racialized environment, predetermination and premeditation are ruling regulations in establishing admissibility: "The boys knew, before he did, that he wasn't going to report this — this incident — these crimes. They were bright enough to know that he would quickly realize how neatly they had boxed him in and thus would keep quiet. If he dared enter a complaint against them they would accuse him of raping the girl. . . . Whose story would be believed?" (Ellison 1995b, 219).

The white perpetrators understand his vulnerability, certain and even dependent that his race will make him more likely the suspect rather than a credible legal witness to their attack as easily as the teacher understands it himself. He's the only black teacher in the white town, hired to represent the well-intentioned integrationist efforts of the town. He is a consequence of a postmodern Jim Crowism, the complex scaffolding of affirmative action. In fact, if Warren's thesis were to hold regarding the boundaries of black fiction, this 1971 short story would have no racial currency. Its events occur past the timeline he proposes. But this teacher bears witness to the pernicious persistence of this particular sociolegal racialized conundrum as much as to a vicious criminal act. Petry meticulously crafts this story, and every element—from the migration of the protagonist from the segregated South to a North he would help to integrate, to the crime he witnesses—has a decided racial mooring. Prior to this brutal crime, Dr. Shipley is a testimonial to a social invention—he is a "credit to the race" who has furthered the cause of integration with his employment in the all-white community of Wheeling, New York. Shipley makes certain his appearance fits his appointed duty, indulging in an extraordinary luxury, purchasing a five-hundred-dollar coat from a store in New York City. Retired as a professor of English from the Virginia College for Negroes, he would be the town's first black teacher and certainly, from a reader's perspective, overqualified for the position as a high school English teacher. But the mission is what matters, and he makes certain his appearance matches the gravitas of his integrationist task. He rationalizes the extravagance of his purchase. The coat, with a collar of black Persian lamb, would at least allow his students "to respect my clothes even if they didn't respect my learning" (Petry 1995, 206). Later, in the midst of the terrifying confrontation with the white boys, the same overcoat "immobilized him and the steady pressure of the fur collar against his windpipe was beginning to interfere with his . . . breathing" (214). The horrific scene has all of the requisite imagery and the physical sensation of a lynch mob. Dr. Shipley feels the coat as if it is a lynch rope around his neck and he is the (black Persian) lamb having been led to slaughter.

Despite the story's initial pastoral setting "a full moon [that] lay low on the horizon. . . . [that] gave a wonderful luminous quality to the snow, to the church and to the branches of the great elms dark against the winter sky" (205), its threat eventually overwhelms. Dr. Shipley leaves his teaching job and returns to Virginia resolving that "when he got back . . . he would give the coat away, his pleasure in it destroyed now for he would always remember the horrid feel of the collar tight across his throat" (220).

Petry's is certainly not a story about slavery, nor is it a Jim Crow fiction. Instead, it employs the intentionality of its setting in an integrationist post–Jim Crow era in which the fruits of the civil rights era and its legal battles should have an evident social consequence. After all, the teacher secures his job precisely because of the district's decision to move forward with integration. But the mark of race persists. His body bears evidence that he is still liable at least to the memory of slavery's lynch legacy, a relative of the *Amistad* and the *Antelope*'s human cargo. Like Morrison's rememory, Petry's figural reminder of lynching illustrates how slavery's shackles and vulnerabilities emerge as psychic and/or physical manifestations in the novels of the black tradition well past the era of enslavement. The teacher would certainly have evidence that could have been legally admissible, though likely challenged. He is muted, silenced, precisely because his *visible* blackness constitutes the racialized utility practiced by whites and blacks alike. The juridical frame Petry has selected for this instrumental racialism seems as persistent as the fiction that recalls it and constitutes the kind of evidentiary racial remains that characterize the tradition.

In fact, it is precisely this version of juridical racial instrumentality that has become brutally predictable. In 1994, with a perverse and practiced ease, a young white South Carolina mother, Susan Smith, could make the false claim that her car was hijacked and her children drowned by a black man.[13] Despite what would be our desiderata, the modern era does not displace the association of race, crime, and law. Legal boundedness is not merely a lingering badge or incident of slavery. Post–Jim Crow era America inevitably displays its penumbral presence. Precedent is practice.

Black Legibility — Can I Get a Witness?

Race exerts evidentiary authority with regard to its suture of legal rights to persons whose bodies had to be "made right" and literally written into legal being. Race is the evidentiary detritus of the constitution's regard of property and subsequently regulates the rights that extend to (the composition of) constitutionally cognizable persons. It is striking to review the prolific literary scenes that seem to offer the body up to the reader/adjudicator as evidence of the claim it makes that has been nullified even after the compelling metaphor of slavery as a narrative machine dissipates.

In Gloria Naylor's *Linden Hills*, Willa Nedeed carries the dead body of her son up the stairs on Christmas Eve, bearing witness to his death. The decomposing evidence of her child's body is her proof of generational link to the father who has disowned him and imprisoned Willa because the child's color did not match his father's.[14]

In Randall Kenan's *Visitation of Spirits*, the boy Horace, chased by the unboundedness of his sexuality and complicated by the conservatism of racial regulation in his church, offers his own body as sacrifice — arguably evidence of the disembodiment of his torture.[15] The book grasps the mystic potential of the myth and spiritual "soon one morning when this life is over, I'll fly away" as Horace imagines himself a bird, freed from "the *rules* [that] were too hard for me to keep" (Kenan 1987, 250, my emphasis). He describes the aftermath of his suicide — "the day did not stop in its tracks: clocks did not stop. The school buses rolled . . . faces were washed . . . food was eaten. And that night the sun set with full intention of rising on the morrow" (254) — understanding how the evidentiary trauma of his life was invisible to the quotidian events of the day. His own misery was contextualized as evidence of things not seen.

Stephen Carter's *New England White* foregrounds the political legal foundations of this country in a mystery that creates a synergy from the intersection of race, class, and access that is crucial to the novel's unfolding.[16] The seemingly intact upper-class black family begins to come undone when "that colored professor got himself killed in November" (Carter 2007, 3) and the college president's (former White House counsel's) wife recognizes the dead man as a former lover. The color-coded politics that shape Carter's legal thriller are narrativized against evolving proofs, inferences, and arguments that are the stuff of evidence as well as the thick potential of racialized narratives. And the main character's name, Lemaster, points rather obviously to the history of enslavement that seems just a spirit-space away from the told story in this fiction.

Richard Wright's posthumously released *A Father's Law* is, in my judgment, a compelling legal thriller.[17] The solution to the crime that the newly appointed black police chief must solve—a series of murders in a white suburb of Chicago—lead him to suspect his son, who studies sociology at the University of Chicago. Is the son also a murderer acting out, as did Wright's Bigger Thomas in *Native Son*, an alternative version of the racial tragedies his color make inevitable?[18] Is the son's confession to the crime the novel's truth or does it fit into the offered pattern of false confessions that have also been his habit? The father's judgment depends on evidence—including a bit of cement on the boy's shoe that matches that from one of the crime scenes. The book seems a workmanlike legal procedure, but then comes the puzzlement of his son's confession to the crime that must also be read in the context of previous statements he had made, claiming responsibility for crimes he could not have committed. The laws of evidence make the pattern of his conduct and the physical evidence admissible. And they are contradictory. Which is the fact of this matter?

> "Those two samples of cement you sent over the lab," Lieutenant Parrish reported. "Well they are the same. There's no doubt about it."
> "That's what I figured . . ."
> "And our lab reports that it is the same cement?"
> "Yeah. . . ."
> "Ed, I'm going crazy! My son's no murderer! But the facts are here. Jesus, the chief of police's son is the criminal that is captured! Is this a joke? Is somebody playing a goddamn trick on me? Well, it isn't funny,

Goddamnit. Was that stunt about Tommy pretending that he was a robber *true?*" (Wright 2008, 263)

In other words, is his son's pretense the fiction, or is his confession a fact? The confusion of rules regarding kinship, race, and desire interfere, leaving the novel's ending at least inconclusive if not indeterminable.

In *Native Son*, prosecutors allow the witness on the stand, the coroner, to testify in the presence of the body of Bigger Thomas's murdered black girlfriend Bessie Mears. Bigger raped and then bludgeoned her to death when he realized she would be a threat to the discovery of the crime he had committed in killing white heiress Mary Dalton.[19] Bessie was Bigger's (or Wright's) necessarily disposable evidence. The deputy coroner announces, "I have decided to offer in evidence the raped and mutilated body of one Bessie Mears, and the testimony of police officers and doctors relating to the cause and manner of her death" (Wright 2005, 330). But it was not justice for Bessie that the coroner sought in offering her body to the courtroom, instead:

> "It will enable the jury to determine the exact manner of the death of Mary Dalton, who was slain by the man who slew Bessie Mears!" the coroner said in a scream that was compounded of rage and vindictiveness. . . . Bigger was crushed, helpless. His lips dropped wide apart. . . . He had completely forgotten Bessie during the inquest of Mary. He understood what was being done. To offer the dead body of Bessie as evidence and proof that he had murdered Mary would make him appear a monster; it would stir up more hate against him. . . . Though he had killed a black girl and a white girl, he knew that it would be for the death of the white girl that he would be punished. The black girl was merely "evidence." (330–331)

A stylistic imaginary gestures toward an earlier black American literature that argued the proof of the body was proof of humanity. But this argument has evolved to represent that body's elite literary accomplishments might also stand as evidence of an especially well-qualified humanity. In

BookMarks, I write, "Once the assumption of literacy was no longer the sole mark of an 'exceptional Negro,' black authors found a way to signal their authority [with] detailed and specific lists of the books they had read. . . . It registered as a claim to having mastered the best of the intellectual habits of an educated elite" (Holloway 2006, 9). In fact and perhaps as a legacy of this bookmarking habit, writing and text play critical compositional roles in black fiction.

Naylor's Willa Nedeed reads notes scribbled in the pages of a Bible in her basement prison. They are recipes and clues to her membership in a lineage of Nedeed wives, all of whom were imprisoned by the contractual obligations of the marriage. At the story's end, although the texts she discovers are evidence of the malevolent Nedeeds' selectivity and breeding of their wives to produce children that looked like the father, it is the child's body she carries up from the basement, leaving the documentary evidence of the texts to burn in the fire that will consume the house. The fire is reminiscent of John Washington's immolation of his own obsessive, academically inclined note taking in order to discover the truth of the matter of the death of the Chaneysville thirteen. Professor Washington finally listens to the testimonial voice of Old Jack rather than rely on the ledger his father left, or the professional notes he had compiled. In *Native Son*, Bessie Mears' "still oblong white draped form under the sheet on the [court room's] table" (Wright 2005, 331) displaces spoken testimony but still serves as evidence. Her body was literally what remained. Mary Dalton's body had been burned — its textual privacies arguably protected from the public display in the courtroom. In Alice Walker's *The Color Purple* letters that Celie exchanges with her sister Nettie expose their truth:[20] "My daddy lynch. My mama crazy. All my half-brothers and sisters no kin to me. My children not my sister and brother. Pa not pa" (Walker 2006, 173). Even with the clarity of this epistolary evidence, a narrative pairing of text and body is still necessary. What she wants to know is where her real father is buried — "for the first time in my life I wanted to see Pa" (174). For Celie, her father's body would be dispositive — the evidence that might liberate the sisters from the fiction of incest that has tortured them. The evidentiary pattern of bodies as and bodies accompanied by text is repeated in Morrison's twenty-first-century novel *Paradise*, where Patricia, also a teacher, echoes the performance of David Bradley's professor. Patricia has attempted to document the town's confusing generations—looking for a link to the unstated regulations that govern the conduct of the ruling families in a genealogy she carefully composes in black and white composition notebooks. Eventually, she finds Professor Washington's solution to be hers as well. She burns her books and scraps of records:

> Fifteen minutes later Pat stood in the garden. . . . No wind to speak of, so the fire in the oil barrel was easily contained. One by one she dropped cardboard files, sheets of paper—both stapled and loose—into the flames. She had to tear the covers off the composition notebooks and hold them slant with a stick so they would not smother the fire. The smoke was bitter. . . . It took some time, but finally she turned her back on the ashes and walked into her house. . . . At the kitchen sink she washed her hands and dashed water on her face. She felt clean. Perhaps that was why she began to laugh. Lightly at first and then heavily, her head thrown back as she sat at the table. Did they really think they could keep this up? The numbers, the bloodlines, the who fucks who? All those generations of 8-rocks kept going, just to end up narrow as bale wire? Well, to stay alive maybe they could. Maybe they should *since nobody dies in Ruby*. (Morrison 1998, 215–216, my emphasis)

Richard Perry's *Montgomery's Children* uses the same mythology of a town where nobody dies as a site for storytelling. Both Morrison and Perry suggest that the black body's vitality is evidence of something more—and when mortality catches up to the towns that have protected themselves from the patterns of racism, funerals become the space where a composed ritual takes hold and prospers. When Morrison's novel repeats the signifying and evolutionary authority of the body as "nobody dies in Ruby," the absence of death forms a critical relationship to documentary record.

Black bodies develop evidentiary authority in order to tell an alternative story. Richard Wright's Bessie was, after all, "merely evidence."

In each of these examples, it is as if the prejudicial presence of the body, tortured, dead, dismembered, or otherwise disordered, was evidentiary material more important than the probative value of text. When Dana, in Octavia Butler's *Kindred* successfully returns to the present having altered her enslaved past to assure her future, she actually loses a part of her body in the transference. "I lost an arm on my last trip home. My left arm" (Butler 2004, 9). Her husband Kevin is worried that he might be implicated in her injury; but she reassures him, "They're sure I did it, but there were no witnesses" (10). It's a legalism that matters. Even though the severed arm is missing—caught somewhere in a maelstrom of events that is metaphysically inexplicable, and despite the abundance of text that attempts that very explanation. "I told as much of the truth as I could" (11), Kevin explains; it is the missing limb that is the evidence the story holds—both in its absence and in the horror the disembodiment represents.

Critical to the focus on the black body is the status and integrity of the black body as property or as persons. The cases of the *Antelope* and the *Amistad* harbinger this relatedness—especially once we realize that, as these cases wound their way through the courts, the numbers of Africans who literally survived until adjudication was markedly reduced from the original bodies that mattered.

Trying to Read Me

The idea of the admissibility, the value of evidence and the exchange between probative and prejudicial values is critical to an understanding of the bridge it plays in the constitution of race as a legal fiction. One is always in contest with the other. Sometimes that contestatory space is the literary objective. Like the scales of justice deployed so frequently in legal narrative, the necessity of both potentials is an inclusive and complex necessity. One exists in relation to the other. Black literatures of the United

States consistently explore the relatedness between body and text, making it unnecessary for the physical body to "win" the evidentiary battle. Prejudice can be a critically rich terrain to explore, and probative value regarding the truth of the matter is more often a value that unleashes a complex web of truths. In *Beloved*, Sethe's chokecherry sketch of scars on her back is evidence of the brutality she has endured. Her body becomes text. Recalling this intextuation of the body assists our reading of the brief but critically significant trial in Hurston's *Their Eyes Were Watching God* as less an exploration of what evidence might render Janie culpable for Tea Cake's death than an interrogation of the survival of Janie's body as having evidentiary value. Sherley Anne Williams's *Dessa Rose* claims a similar place in this literary inscribing of the body.[21] In that text, as in *Beloved*, the inalienability of text from body explains the suture of the two evidentiary values that carry an always available legal inscription. In *Dessa Rose*, Dessa's whipped, branded, inscribed body would betray her enslaved status. Dessa's efforts to hide that text, to withhold herself from evidence, is a maneuver intimately composed within the potential of legal repercussions. Nehemiah, the writer who hopes to profit from a book about Dessa's story as a slave awaiting execution accused of killed white men and leading a group of slaves into rebellion, takes up the role of the professor/teacher/finder of fact. "The law need proof, Nemi say" (Williams 2010, 229). When Dessa leaves the sheriff's office, Nehemiah attempts to assert the textual authority he's been composing:

> "I know its her . . . I got her down here in my book." And he reach and took out that little black-bound pad he wrote in the whole time I knowed him. . . . Clara reached for the book and knocked it out his hand. The pages wasn't bound in the cover and they fell out, scattering about the floor. Nemi started grabbing the papers, pushing them in the sheriff's hand. . . . "Nemi, ain't nothing but some scribbling on here," sheriff say. "Can't no one read this." (231–232)

The legible failure that allows Dessa's escape was her success at keeping them from "under her dress"—keeping private and illegible the script of scars on her body that would otherwise be read into the law and lead to her execution. Later, Dessa reflects on the memory her body carries, a text that would betray her: "I never will forget Nemi *trying to read me*" (236, my emphasis).

The theoretical landscape of evidentiary values that surface in the black text and in the black body as text lies in the inexplicably persistent value of things not seen, the escape of narratives or the fugitivity of bodies that compose them from the kind of notice that would, if discernible or visible, give them evidentiary value. Recall, for example, how the *Invisible Man*'s opening narrative begins with an insistent testimonial explaining that he is present but unseen. The opening prologue to the novel is an intensely physical explication of his ontological claim. Nevertheless, when it comes to a question of law, he is invisible, a direct opposition to a legal cognizability. As a black man, he is unrecognizable. He is even an outlaw from the inscription of criminality. In the same way that the *Amistad*'s Spanish claimants wanted the enslaved to be legally named as "murderers" so that they might be persons rather than property, the crimes of an Invisible Man are unregulated. Biosocialities depend on visibility, something Ellison's novel declares, in its first line, as outside of the boundaries of his character: "I am an Invisible Man" (Ellison 1995b, 1). Ironically, the man actually proffers evidence of his de facto unrecognizability through an insistent physicality that is at first corporeal before it is active: "I am a man of substance, of flesh and bone, fiber and liquids — and I might even be said to possess a mind."[22]

The Invisible Man's claim goes straight to the heart of mens rea (from Latin, meaning literally "a guilty mind," but also understood as "criminal intent"), which is, for criminal law, a standard that argues the necessity of the presence of both the criminal act and mens rea. The interesting conundrum for U.S. legalisms, one that Ellison's novel probes, is the failure of U.S. cultures to perceive blacks as human enough to have the capacity to act as reasonable persons. This critical legal standard is one scholar Christine Krueger appropriately recognizes as a "legal fiction of late twentieth century American jurisprudence."[23] Krueger appropriately takes notice of the gendered instantiation of the reasonable man standard. Twentieth-century black fiction is composed with the notion of mens rea intact, whether it exists in Bigger Thomas's otherwise inexplicable (except through the lens of existentialism) brutality. "What I killed for, I am" or the men of *Paradise* who "shoot the white girl first" or Bird's frantic search for evidence of whether or not her white lover who was "too smooth in the face, too untroubled, unscratched, unmarred in any way" murdered her best friend in Thulani Davis's *Maker of Saints*.[24] These explanations for conduct are loops of reasoning that allow mens rea to become the final hurdle for the African American whose constitution is still haunted by the clause that legally fractionalized them.

If the evidentiary matters of twentieth-century literature seem to overwhelm, the precedent for these textual obsessions might be located in a theory of evidence that composes the black person as a fictional legatee of the constitution's originary claim. From this perspective, a metaphysics of embodiment seems a predictable focus for a literature about persons whose legal constitution is in question. And importantly, it locates the question outside of the bodies themselves. Ellison's Invisible Man proclaims, "That invisibility to which I refer occurs because of a peculiar disposition of the eyes of those with whom I come in contact" (2). And then, in order to challenge the metaphysics to which he is assigned, and in case the reader has not understood him as outside of the law, he commits a brutal assault—testified to in a newspaper that "reports" about a man who had been "mugged." If he is not already fugitive, he certainly is with this act. The intense physicality of this act of a vicious mugging is less attended to than his theft of power from Monopolated Power & Light, an event that does lead to a compelling image of this man in a basement cave lit by thousands of light bulbs. And yes, theft and its imagery are certainly important; but if we miss the evidence that leads him to this hiding place it has the oblique standing of evidence of things unseen and he is rendered unreadable, as invisible in the reader's eyes as he is to the people who pass him by. Following this deconstitution, a critical fugitivity sets up the potential for the rest of the text.

In noting the kinds of crimes (adultery, witchcraft) that earned public attention in Victorian England, Christine Krueger writes that "in order to exploit the fear of propertied males, that they, too, could suffer legal erasure and be robbed of their rights as rational agents" (Krueger 2010, 116) the "presumptive loss of credibility that robbed a sane man not only of his civil rights but also of the power to assert his rationality" left a "privileged man" vulnerable to the condition of women (*femes coverts*) "whose protests would be dismissed as delusional ravings."[25] Krueger's is a critically important notation that might encourage a rereading of the Prologue of *Invisible Man* that understands the sociality that is constructed within and through the critical legalism it engages. The man who was the victim of the opening assault was "a tall blond man" who looked at him "insolently out of his blue eyes." This is the owner of a privileged personhood whose very presence makes any rational assertion by the Invisible Man moot. That was why "he kicked him in a frenzy" even as the man "still uttered insults though his lips were frothy with blood." His frenzy was the fury of the unseen.

James Baldwin understood the power in the "evidence of things not seen"—the title he used for his nonfiction narrative of the Atlanta child murders.[26] Although Baldwin's fiction may not have participated in the brutal physicality that Ellison and Wright indulged, Baldwin was similarly engaged in the proof of what Krueger, in a reference to rational realists of British literary history refers to as a "private history" (Krueger 2010, 117).

This private/public dichotomy is a useful bifurcation that clarifies the engagements and insistence of U.S. black literatures in revealing how differential public histories engaged the private, subjective, and oft-times silenced or erased experiences of black Americans. It is not unreasonable to consider these as reasons that these literatures circle back to slavery with such consistency. Enslavement entailed a substantial private history of conduct that the public enactment of laws designed in order to right the history of legal harms even though they could not modify the social structures of those histories. If we wonder at the vitality of enslaved narratives or their generational kin emerging even in twenty-first-century fictions, we might look to the presumptive necessities of legal proof as not only an establishment of a fugitive imagination that could, if documented, gain the status of a record, but a liberal imagination that is indebted to naming its generation — even if that generation is a haunt.

The haunts linger. Alice Walker's Meridian suffers from what we would call today posttraumatic stress. Her catatonia, hair loss, paralysis, and fatigue are directly related to the extraordinary kinds of allegiances required from civil rights workers, including having to ponder whether or not she would kill for the revolution. "Will you kill for the revolution, not just die for it?"[27] Meridian saw herself "held by the past: by the memory of old black men in the South who, caught by surprise in the eye of a camera, never shifted their position but looked directly back" (14). When Walter Mosley's Ptolemy Gray *loses* the chronology of his own life in the pitiful decline that dementia assures (and that loss of time is characteristic of black postmodernism), he also *loosens* a memory of a postslavery Jim Crow era "legal" lynching that would otherwise have been buried in the brutality of the lynch-law ruled South. Mosley's novel is a complex and rich exploration of coherence and incoherence against the backdrop of unspeakable acts, spoken.

Testimonial — whether it is like Janie's courtroom testimony in Hurston's *Their Eyes Were Watching God* where "the court set and Janie saw the judge . . . [a]nd twelve more white men had stopped whatever they were doing to listen and pass on what happened."[28] Thirteen white folks and "all of the colored people standing up in the back of the courtroom" were there to pass judgment. But whites would determine the condition of her life. Certainly the disparity of authority tells one side of this story. But the private thoughts of the black folk, silent but united in their condemnation — "so many were there against her that a light slap from each one of them would have beat her to death" — clarifies the disparity of authority and the public investment in testimonial. Janie embodies a collision and conflation of private body and a public text, an intersectionality that turns on the kind of witness she might be. Notably it is not the substance of Janie's testimonial but her striking physical presence in the courtroom that stands as the evidence that will be adjudicated. It is not an uncommon posturing of the body as evidence.

Consider the way in which Bradley's professor essentially provides a deposition for the testimonial that will become the received truth of the *Chaneysville Incident*. Janie's voice was nullified in her trial, rendered into a third person narrative "she tried to make them see. . . . She didn't plead to anybody. She just sat there and told and when she was through she hushed." As if an acknowledgment that reproducing her spoken words would not have standing, the actual discourse is saved for the narrative of her attorney's summary statement: "Gentlemen of the jury, it is for you to decide whether the defendant has committed a cold blooded murder or whether she is a poor broken creature, a devoted wife trapped by unfortunate circumstances" (Hurston 1998, 155). Nowhere in the judicial instructions is she considered a person, instead she is a "broken *creature*" and a "devoted wife" both allusions to a propertied status—*femes covert* whose rights were dependent on their relationship to their husbands. The broken creature is reminiscent of slavery's fractional bodies whose humanity was in question, and the devoted wife's humanity is further diminished to a status only visible in terms of her relationship to her husband. The potential of liberal agency her freedom might represent is arguably a viable potential of her being found not guilty. Janie does not relinquish herself to the "white women who cried and stood around her like a protecting wall" instead she returns to the black community that has ostracized her. It is certainly an outcome that has the legal potential of attachment to a doctrine of rationality, one that literary and legal scholar Christine Krueger perceptively notices as the authorial agency women novelists hold as potential, even as an appeal to the standard of the rational person that shifts from British common law to U.S. legalisms gains a particular gendered status in the shift of continents. However, the potential of a strategic legalism is complicated when held by a black body—its association with a credible rationality, however that might be gendered, is in U.S. history complicated by the colored construction of the body that would inhabit that rational personhood. The standard of proof that accompanies a proffer of evidence entangles not only the literary character, but, when the author is black, the author's credibility as well. Any potential for a liberal imaginary invested in black authorship depends as much on the standing of the author as it does on the characters that author would create. In fact, the evidentiary foundation of literature's claim is directly tied to the substantive authority of authorial standing. Black writers who engage race operate in complex relationships to texts that explore the metaphysical instabilities inherent in the "black" writer. Hurston's black folk look for a legal judgment that is separable from the kind of indeterminacy evident in an ethical perspective that allows Tea Cake's death to be "accidental and justifiable" in the finding of the jury but a grave injustice in the watchful eyes of the black folks who were, through much of the novel, "watching God." It's as clear an indication of the complex evidentiary terrain that black folks encounter as any in literature. The *ethics* of personhood, of act, and of judgment are necessarily a morality tale; and yet the thick terrain of black life is consistently surrendered as a matter for legal resolution, and the evidence a court of reasonable persons might consider as admissible would eliminate or fix the contradictions inherent in black testimonial.

As much as U.S. black literatures engage the necessity of evidence as historical proof or contemporary legitimacy, there is abundant illustration that the differential adjudication of that proffer is what constructs the literary event. That complexity, or at least the differential potential of literary interpretation, falls directly into fiction's terrains. Consider, as an example, the perfectly reasonable but widely disparate testimony in Nathan McCall's *Them*, a novel about property, gentrification, home ownership, and the view of whether a call to the police will help or hinder a neighborhood argument.[29] Every act in this novel depends on a determination of ownership and rights — or at least the differential judgments attached to ownership and property rights. In McCall's fiction, that depends on who has the authoritative narrative, and that authority is clearly on display at a neighborhood meeting that, if pushed back to the mid twentieth century may have signified the question of incorporation Ralph Ellison engaged in the Prologue of *The Invisible Man*.

> The whites arrived early for the neighborhood meeting. They sat up front, arms folded and legs crossed, confident that, finally, the universe was evolving, as it should. Moments before the meeting was set to start, the faithful few blacks trickled in and headed directly to the back of the room like they had been ordered there. Once seated, some slouched at the ends of aisles, looking dazed, cross, unsure of themselves.
>
> And for good reason. A civic league election had been held the month before. A new league president was put in place. Now it was official: Power in the Old Fourth Ward had changed hands.
>
> The shift, it seemed, had happened overnight. . . .
>
> Later, the black people of the ward ventured outdoors, yoo-hooing at mailboxes and across rickety fences. They asked each other, and themselves, over and over: If the place was wilderness before *they* showed up, then what have *we* been doin here all this time. *Are we then, invisible?* (McCall 2008, 247, my emphasis)

If the right to property or even the right to testify, or to offer evidence, or to be vulnerable to the consequence of that evidentiary offering is differentially valued, the imaginative liberalism one would presume accompanies a fiction becomes, in black fiction, a *liberally imagined* personhood that is always and already a contested site. Here, black literatures consistently find its most provocative material.

The idea of legitimacy becomes an a priori ground for debate. And to the extent that legitimacy, with all of its legal entailments, is a particular origin story for black literatures, it emerges as black literature's changing same, a theory of noticeable aesthetic continuities that I would argue are also noticeably structural and contingent on the changing same of American legal histories with its historically persistent patterns of address and redress of the rights and identities of U.S. blacks.

What Baldwin documented in the Atlanta child murders as the "evidence of things not seen" and what Ellison introduces as the Invisible

Man's brutal dilemma of fugitivity is, ironically, the substance of U.S. black literatures that assures the genre's literary persistence. Alone, the subject matter of enslavement, or colorism, or act, or identitarianisms (those of politics or potential) might easily have the kinds of ebbs and flows of literatures as other sites, like those regional geographies of place that have historically claimed a literary cohesion and the characters, issues, and events that readers have come to recognize as being like, or relational to those associations. The difference that matters is the architecture, the skeleton of U.S. legalisms that have attached, or that have been attached to those substantive matters of identity that the law persistently enforces as a credible means of escaping the very distinctions it seeks to make, ironically, invisible through legal equal protections that only adhere if the difference is outed. Because evidence law depends on admissibility (of statements or objects), the scrutiny attached to testimonial formations (documents or material evidence) that are often at the center of black literatures has a potentially intense relationship to the legal frames in which that testimony joins with a consequential scrutiny of U.S. socialities. Determining the truth of the matter, especially with the standard of a reasonable person, makes a compelling complication of a fiction that depends on an already determined contest between racialized readings of narratives. The substance of those fictions that creatively engage U.S. racialisms cannot help but experience this legal entanglement, but the legal entanglement by itself only offers the framework. Literature's complexities fashion the imaginative project.

In literature, narrative evidence attaches itself to the socialities we practice. Writing of the courtroom that would bring to trial the man eventually convicted of the Atlanta child murders, Baldwin explains the conundrum of the suspension of disbelief Coleridge first attached to fiction, and that the spectacle and site of a courtroom attaches to its processes. It is the place, Baldwin notes, where one is expected to suspend justice. But he also is careful to point out the perplexity of biosocialities that the law implicitly regards when it argues for the habits and traditions of a people being a reasonable standard in constitutional interpretation. In fact, Baldwin comes very near that familiar legal phrasing and the literary reference that Coleridge explained as a "willing suspension of disbelief"[30] when he explains that:

> to suspend judgment demands that one dismiss one's perceptions at the very same moment that one is most crucially—and cruelly—dependent on them. . . . Our ability to perceive is at once tyrannized by our expectations, and at war with them. Our expectations are revealed in our habits, our manner: our defeats, terrors, genuine or imagined triumphs risk being more visible to others than to ourselves." (Baldwin 1995, 1)

When the narratives in black literatures invest in testimony, they seem to do so in order to accomplish the same ends as legal procedures require. The association between the fact of law and the fiction of literature is apparent in the ways in which testimony consistently matters, whether it is Bradley's Old Jack or the letters shared between Nettie and Celie in *The Color Purple.*

The *materia* of evidence—exhibits, testimony, or the (black) bodies in/of evidence—work to establish and discern narrative effect. The stash of treasure in the captain's cabin in Charles Johnson's *Middle Passage* is evidence of his thievery and character; the plague of robins in *Sula*—as enigmatic a symbol as it is figural—is also evidence that accompanies and pronounces her problematic return to the community. A single robin might be a harbinger of spring, but a plague of them is a threat, a lawless infestation. Neo–slave Dessa hides her scars to save her life, civil rights warrior Minnie wonders if she wants to be well, and in *Fledgling*, Octavia Butler's Shori's preteen body belies the fact that she is a fifty-three-year-old vampire whose dark skin is a genetic manipulation designed to protect the "race" of vampires from the sun. As Shori's heritage and her relationships disrupt normative boundaries—sex between children and adults, between races, same sex partners and different genetic variations of humans—Butler helps us to probe what identity might mean, and more important, what it means to be human in an (arguably) postracial era.[31]

Race sustains its narrative weight in fiction for the same reasons that it persists in our societies. Black writers who write the racial text engage the sociolegal history of evidentiary substance that reflects and enmeshes the habits and traditions of our everyday lives.

THREE

Composing Contract

I'm not a racist. I just don't believe in mixing the races that way.
I have piles and piles of black friends. They come to my home, I marry
them, they use my bathroom. I treat them just like everyone else.

— (former) Judge Keith Bardwell, justice of the peace,
Tangipahoa Parish, Louisiana, November 2009

A contract is a legal form of a promise.[1] In law, contracts are deeply regulated. They are governed by the principle of consideration (the value in the exchange), by obligation, representation, disclosure, and even fairness. In fact, with this constellation of duties, the law of contract may be the one area of law that most directly incorporates and composes complexities inherent in compelling narratives. A contract may even be judged as illusory. It has all the components of a fiction.

When Justice Keith Bardwell refused to issue a license that would allow the interracial couple to enter a contractual relationship of marriage, they were essentially preempted from enjoying the legal version of the promise they wanted to make with each other. Instead, Bardwell shrouded their inquiry in a century of biosocialities regarding disease and contagion, friendships with and without racial boundaries, and a flawed notion of equal treatment ("I treat them like anybody else").

I bring together the contemporary (for this writing) Louisiana event in the epigraph to this chapter alongside the regulation of law and society with respect to the enforceable nature of a promise in order to indicate the ways in which the racialized versions of contractual promises become the stuff of fiction. Lorraine Hansberry certainly took advantage of this particular utility in her critically acclaimed drama *A Raisin in the Sun* that was based on her own family's purchase of a home in Chicago covered by a neighborhood covenant that was exclusionary to blacks. Her family's experience was actually more complicated than the drama. When white homeowners complained that the covenant was violated with the Hansberry's purchase, the NAACP assisted Carl Hansberry's legal challenge of the covenant and the subsequent 1940 Supreme Court narrow ruling in *Hansberry v. Lee* invalidated the court's 1926 ruling in *Corrigan v. Buckley* that upheld the legality of racial covenants. *Hansberry v. Lee* would become a critical precedent for the federal ruling in *Shelley v. Kraemer*, which declared the unconstitutionality of all racial housing covenants.[2]

However, Bardwell's twenty-first century refusal to issue the interracial couple the right to enter into a marriage contract indicates that not all contractual promises are judiciously managed. I don't just want to relay the strange set of bedfellows this judge went mining for in proving the interconnectedness of his ignorance and his lack of bad intent (friends, bathrooms, home visits) but instead want to underscore how the ultimate issue here is the racialized potential of matters essentially unrelated to legal reasoning but nonetheless clearly directing his legal intervention. This clarifies a background of social issues that constituted Jim Crowed facilities and laws that prevented interracial marriages and the ways in which the legal composition of arguments that might extend or not extend the constitutional right to enter into a contract were also "governed" by the shadow of racial reasoning. In the AP story that took the local issue nationwide, the press reports the justice's concern was for the potential children from the contractual marriage he had a judicial obligation to enforce: "He has discussed the topic with blacks and whites, along with witnessing some interracial marriages. He came to the conclusion that most of black society does not readily accept offspring of such relationships, and neither does white society, he said. 'There is a problem with both groups accepting a child from such a marriage,' Bardwell said. 'I think those children suffer and I won't help put them through it.'"

Bardwell's language is almost identical to the legal defense mounted in *Loving v. Virginia* where the state expresses its concerns regarding the potential of interracial marriages as concerns about the children from these unions. On April 10, 1967, state attorney R. D. McIlwaine spoke for the state of Virginia in oral argument to the Supreme Court:

> It is the family which constitutes the structural element of society. . . . The state has a natural, direct and vital interest in maximizing the number of successful marriages which lead to stable homes and families and in minimizing those which do not. . . . It is clear from the most recently available evidence on the psycho-sociological aspect of this question that inter-married families are subjected to much greater pressures and problems. The state's prohibition stands on same footing as polygamous marriage, incestuous marriage [and the] . . . prevention of the marriage of people who are mentally incompetent. . . . It is not infrequent that the children of inter-married parents are referred to not as the children of inter-married parents but as . . . the victims of inter-married parents, and the martyrs of intermarried parents.[3]

The shadow of civil wrongs perpetrated through the law is a lingering and penumbral matter in legal parlance, and it is intimately linked with a persistent and virulently pejorative imaginary regarding the black body—a fear of its physical characteristics and the consequences of race "mixing." R. D. McIlwaine's Supreme Court argument explained how "intermarriage . . . causes a child to have insuperable difficulties in identification [that] no child can come to without damage to himself." If we recall Cheryl Harris's argument referenced in chapter 1 of this book regarding the social and legal value in perpetuating whiteness as something desirable and precious, some of this fear begins to make a perverse sense. As useful and as frustrating as it may be to spend time with deconstructing the biases and ignorance in this man's actions, I'd like readers to take note of the era in which Bardwell's concern was expressed — well into the presidency of a biracial man who seems to have done quite well for himself as the child of parents of different nationalities and races. There's some facial evidence, in other words, that Mr. Bardwell's thinking is flawed. But this flaw is not the legal failure. That failure is his lack of regard of the regulatory federal decision (the holding in *Loving*) that established that blacks and whites (at the writing of this book, interpreted as heterosexual couples) had identical marriage rights.[4] Using a historically grounded bias that his decision was made to benefit children who had not even been conceived, who could not, in fact, even stand as persons in the eye of the law, Bardwell refused the couple a license that would allow them to enter into the contract of marriage.[5]

The issues of this chapter focus on the legal synonymy between contract and promise. It illustrates how black literatures place race at the center of contested obligations and how these racialized entanglements find their way to the law. At the end of 2012, the right to marriage was still contested in the courts with regard to whom the right extends and whether it is fundamental and federal, or a right of states to grant or deny. The precedent in this matter of same sex marriage is quite clearly, for some legal theorists, set in the 1967 case *Loving v. Virginia*, where the Supreme Court overruled any extant state statues that forbade marriage between couples of different races.[6] But the laws of equity and citizenship established with the civil rights amendments did not end the legal question over the social situations of race. And literature similarly found interracialisms a fecund site for literary drama and intrigue — not simply in the era of slavery, or the early century when books like Nella Larsen's *Passing* whispered a reference to the "Rhinelander matter."[7] It was a loud whisper that echoed wide and deep.

In his review of Larsen's novella, without the precocity that has been attached to his prediction of the twentieth century's problem being the color line, W.E.B. Du Bois wrote: "It is all a petty, silly matter of no real importance which another generation will comprehend with great difficulty. But today, and in the minds of most white Americans, it is a matter of tremendous moral import. One may deceive as to killing, stealing and adultery, but you must tell your 'friend' that you're 'colored,' or suffer a very material hell fire in this world, if not in the next."[8]

To the contrary of this "petty matter" having literary interest only within the generation of Du Bois, Mr. Bardwell has indicated that inter-racial marriages and/or sexual relationships are contemporary conflicted sites, and novels like Alice Walker's *Meridian*, Octavia Butler's, *Kindred*, and even for Toni Morrison's much maligned *Sula*, who is finally and fully disowned when the rumor spreads that she sleeps with white men, proves the narrative remains a compelling reason for the community's shunning. These three late-twentieth-century novels urge the same question that prompted earlier, enslaved-era analyses. This span of decades begs the question why and how does race still matter? Why aren't these settled questions for law and disinterested foci in literature and society?

"A novel-like tenor"

The fact that these questions are still relevant in U.S. black literatures parallels their relevance also in the legal lives of Americans. At least, the couple in Tangipahoa Parish, Louisiana, who sought a marriage contract found this to be the case in 2009. And it seemed that justice of the peace was quite explicit in his worry about the progeny. If we look back in history, the legal standard is definitively attached to the question of who carries forward, or loses, the value attached to some persons, especially to the extent that racial distinctiveness seems to threaten racial privilege.

Louisiana courts' jurisdiction regarding race and identity persisted long past the era of slavery. In 1955, Robert Green filed suit (*Green v. City of New Orleans*) to change the race on the birth certificate of a four-year-old girl, Jacqueline Henley.[9] Green was the Negro foster parent of the little girl. During the legal processes attached to his petition, the child's birth certificate was obtained. She had been categorized as white. An interracial adoption would not be legal, and when his petition was denied Green appealed.

The details of the case are somewhat complex, but discoverable from court records. Jacqueline was being raised by her aunt. Her birth mother — who had given the child to her sister to raise during her illness — died shortly after the aunt asked the Department of Welfare to take over her care. Her aunt was concerned because "neighbors were beginning to comment about the medium brown color of the child's skin." She told a welfare worker, Mrs. Oberholtzer, that "she would like the agency to make plans for the child since she felt that she was a Negro and she could no longer keep her in the house; the child was growing darker day by day" and that "remarks were passed that the child was possibly a nigger."[10] The welfare department did carry out the aunt's wishes and mandated that the child's status be changed to "abandoned" allowing Jacqueline's entry into the foster care system. Not without irony, given the claims of the case, she was placed into a Negro foster home where her foster parents, the Greens, eventually pursued a petition to adopt her. Their effort was impeded when it was discovered that the Bureau of Vital Affairs had listed her racial designation as white. The bureau's refusal to change that designation led to Green's appeal.

Adoption is a legal contract. It confers the authority and responsibility that govern and establish a legal relationship between persons. In that sense, adoption is like marriage. Both legal relationships would be subject to a court's interest in preserving a social normativity that conferred privilege on whiteness. Hence the number of state laws that stratified marriage between the races almost always prevented intermarriage between blacks and whites, and sometimes also regulated marriages between whites and Indigenous Americans and whites and Asians. The common denominator in these regulations was always whiteness — a repeating factor that meant judicial interest was directed toward any potential racial admixture that might undermine the integrity of legal whiteness. Recall that naturalization legislation consistently preserved the language of "white persons" even as it evolved to add persons from other "racial" categories as entitled to the benefits of citizenship. In doing so, the law maintained whiteness as the explicit legal standard.

In adoption law, the regulations followed the cautions visible in marriage regulations. Although it was social practice more than legislative action that regulated these matters, when the courts intervened, it was fairly easy to discern how their caution weighed on the side of preserving whiteness. In the *Green* case the courts found a legal reasoning that would not deprive Jacqueline of an identity that was clearly preferential. It was helpful, and arguably determinative, that the state's Bureau of Vital Statistics already legally declared she was white. In rendering their judgment, despite what one could argue was compelling evidence of her visible coloring, the judges chose to rely on the expert testimony of an anthropologist who testified that Jacqueline's race wouldn't be clear until "the child was more developed and mature" deciding that other testimony regarding her current appearance, her aunt's concern, the neighbors' gossip, and the habits of her deceased mother to keep company with Negroes was "hearsay, inferences and presumptions of fact."[11]

Just as the *Loving* court would hear a decade later, evidence from social science "research" was pulled into the testimony. In the *Green* case, an anthropologist's expert testimony decided that phenotype was developmental, and although there seemed to be at least enough melanin for neighbors to question Jacqueline's membership in the white race, that anthropologist determined it was not enough to be ultimately determinative. A decade later, a Jewish rabbi's book would form the basis for Virginia's argument against intermarriage in *Loving v. Virginia*. The rabbi's research was introduced to the court as "definitive," and the court accepted his credentials that included an M.A. in sociology and a Ph.D. in social anthropology as appropriate for rendering expert judgment in this matter.[12] The state's evidence would not lead to its victory. However, in *Green*'s ruling for the state, the court cited the anthropologist's "expert" testimony. The court's ruling made apparent that what seemed to be the (colored) fact of her appearance was not their overriding concern. Instead, their interest was in protecting a state's right to nominate race and its consequential responsibility to that nomination. Their action may be read as a way of extending protection of that identity from the vulnerable space that adoption by a black family and subsequent loss of the privilege of whiteness might entail.

The court's opinion in *Green v. City of New Orleans* opened with this comment: "We feel compelled to remark at the inception of this opinion that we were completely fascinated by the *novel-like* tenor of this record" (emphasis mine).[13] Fiction's potential was clear, and nearly three score years later, Judge Bardwell's renaming his prejudice as a concern for the social welfare of mixed-race children was fully imagined and, at least as far as historical precedent might allow, a legally bound narrative.

It is not the case that the implicit or explicit involvement of legal matters or legal references became an intentional trope selected by black authors because they were poets bid to sing a black song. Instead the ease with which law transmuted into literature was the consequence of the identitarian-bound nature of narrative. When black authors made black folks the subject of their narratives, the ways in which a raced identity was socially maintained followed, and that maintenance was a consequence of the law's persistent interest in making race matter. The fact that the legal cases continued to have a "novel-like tenor" was also consequential. Once race became conferrable, the associated narratives became more and more complex—precisely the stuff of fiction.

Passing and Protection

Among the most riveting cases that would illustrate these matters of subversion, implicit accusation, and thinly concealed racial fears occurred in 1924. The Rhinelander case has been elegantly narrated in Elizabeth Smith-Pryor's book *Property Rites*, in which she focuses on the issue of the property of the black woman's body that was at the center of this case.[14] Smith-Pryor's subtitle gives away the complex narratives that are at issue. *Passing and the Protection of Whiteness* gestures back to Cheryl Harris's seminal essay on "Whiteness as Property." Their shared vocabularies reveal the persistent entanglement of the legal issues of property as/and race. Knowing a bit more about the legal question before the Rhinelander court gives us a critical insight into how the law was used as a promissory note — a contract that would protect the social value of whiteness and use that implicit privilege as a standard.

The basic parameters of the case were widely circulated in the news of the era. The salacious letters shared between the two lovers Leonard (Kip) Rhinelander and Alice Jones were circulated as (pink) supplements that newsboys offered to men for special purchase (they cost five cents more than the newspapers). The case is certainly a narrative that contains all the thick dimensions necessary for a riveting fiction. Kip Rhinelander married Alice Jones, a very light-skinned girl whose mother was white and British and whose father was brown-skinned and British — an immigrant from the West Indies. It seems obvious from the details of the case that Kip knew his bride's "colored" lineage; he spent a good deal of time at her home. As in the Green case, courts allowed into evidence neighborhood, school, and church affiliations to make judgments regarding racial identities when that identity was in dispute.[15] There was, in other words, precedent for the patterns of racial discovery.

Rhinelander was the son of a wealthy white New Yorker, who, upon discovering his son's marriage, threatened to disown him. At first Kip was reluctant to abandon his new bride but eventually his father and his father's lawyers impressed the importance of the matter to him, an importance that undoubtedly brought up the matters of protecting the Rhinelander name and the family's wealth. In a reading of these matters of race, sex, and desire in the nineteenth century, scholar Jeffory Clymer writes that "inheritance . . . is the moment when familial lines are most purposefully drawn, where . . . the inexorable codes defining legal families confronted the private histories of sex and emotion. Because race was a primary way of delimiting who could count as family . . . scenarios of inheritance were regularly formed along and by the color line. . . . Almost as a palimpsest, is the history of family, which has itself been given form by the legal construction and management of racial difference."[16] Clymer's astute reading of the nineteenth century becomes even more substantial by the time these issues reached the twentieth century. If those laws regarding family economies mattered in the 1800s, they had even more potency as the era progressed.

When Leonard agreed to seek an annulment to protect the Rhinelanders' "scenario of inheritance," his new bride—Alice Jones Rhinelander—contested. After a series of different claims by the defendant and claimant, the case eventually settled on her stipulation that she was indeed "colored." Kip argued that he had not known this to be the case before they were married. His counter was that she'd deliberately deceived him into believing that she was white. With that, the legal issue before the court became fraudulent contract, and the evidence they needed to accumulate would go directly toward whether or not he would reasonably have known she was of colored descent. This focus led to extraordinarily intimate testimony. Their letters to each other, describing premarital hotel room trysts, were read into the record before they were printed and sold on New York City's streets.

The implicit issue that motivated the husband's interests was the matter of progeny—who would stand to inherit the Rhinelander fortune if the couple were to have legitimate heirs? Smith-Pryor explains the matter, tying in the notion of property as a value that lay in persons and in things like an inheritance if the marriage produced "mixed-race children who were legally acknowledged as heirs of their parents and families" (2009, 93). Critically related to this was the threat of passing itself—that there could possibly be children or adult persons so light skinned that ordinary citizens might be duped. Smith-Pryor explains that "passing could be perceived as an attempt to steal, by lying about one's true race, the status and benefits of whiteness, the rights of first-class citizenship" (93). The stakes in this matter were so high, both for the Rhinelander family and white society generally, that it produced one of the most startling moments in judicial history when, in a courtroom in New Rochelle, New York, Alice Rhinelander's attorney requested the court's permission for his client to disrobe from the neck to her waist. She did so in judges' chambers, in view of members of the all white jury, the court recorder, the presiding judge, and Alice Rhinelander's mother. The second startling moment in this remarkable case occurred when she won the case. A sociolegal interpretation of the court's decision in Alice's favor factually protected what the jury determined was society's greater need to assure itself that black and white were indeed distinguishable, and especially that the nation's legal system could discern the difference even if some men and women might claim to be unable to make this critical discernment. However, a jury of reasonable persons, as they would have seen themselves to be, could do precisely that. In other words, the victory to Mrs. Alice Rhinelander was a victory for the preservation and protection of the propertied value in whiteness. In *Private Bodies* I explain the competing claims, noting that although "the jury's decision inverted social expectations of race, gender, and privilege—which would have argued for Kip's success. . . . [t]he Rhinelander outcome was intimately related to how deeply, even how quixotically significant these matters of color and discernment were to the social order" (Holloway 2011, 40).

The case is absolutely fascinating for its extraordinary and unprecedented display of a black woman's body as evidence (it was her nipples that the court wanted to see, the presumption of the era being that a white woman's nipples would be pink) and also because of the fact that a poor black defendant won her case against a wealthy and powerful white family.[17] But the values the court upheld are easily associated with the habits and traditions that U.S. legalisms considered. Visible whiteness was amongst the critical values the law would protect in order to defer to the habits and traditions of a country that had come to attach economic value to whiteness. Certainly the Rhinelander matter was a case about property as indicated in the title (*Property Rites*) of Smith-Pryor's book. But it also literally exposed the nation's dependence on the evidentiary and presumptively discoverable characteristics of race. It is a loophole of biologized identity that still exerts it stranglehold today.

The issue of contract is important as well and rests on the intimacy of promises, the vows a couple might have personally shared that became legally actionable when they asked the state to recognize these promises within a contract of marriage. The claim of fraudulent contract that formed the legal question before the court sutures this case to the kinds of rights that legal black bodies earned when they became citizens. The plaintiff's claim that Alice had entered into a fraudulent contract of marriage when she married Kip, and that that fraud was a substantive and deliberate misrepresentation of her color and lineage—a misrepresentation she knew would be material to his decision to marry her—collects property, evidence, and contract back into the triad that this book instantiates as interdependent (and arguably determinative) in the association between law, literature, and race. In declaring the Rhinelander/Jones marriage as valid, the court also declared Alice Rhinelander's identity as a married woman as both visible and legally binding. The consequence of that kind of declarative power is certainly a thick fictive terrain.

For example, the issue in Gayl Jones's *Corregidora* was a marriage that was abusive and damaging. Here, the contract of marriage gained with freedom from the slavemaster Covey's vicious rape that tortured generations of Corregidora women provided no sanctuary to Ursa. In Johnson's *Middle Passage*, the potential of marriage was the threat that led to Rutherford's "escape" to the *Republic*, a ship that turned out to be a slave ship—an alternative form of the legal bondage that would have occurred had he married Isadora in the narrative's opening pages.

The secreted race of Irene's friend Clare in Nella Larsen's *Passing* is a threat not only to the black community, but it's damaging and dangerous to high-society Harlem residents whose friendships were unknown to her husband—a white man who hated "niggers" but had a perplexing—and to the 'colored' women in the room—an offensive habit of calling his wife "Nig." He explains to her perplexed and secretly offended guests who are themselves, masquerading as white women friends of his wife, Clare: "'Well you see, it's like this. When we were first married, she was as white as—as—well as white as a lily. But I declare she's gettin' darker and darker. I tell her if she don't look out, she'll wake up one of these days and find she's turned into a nigger.' He roared with laughter" (2004, 31). Buried in this awkward moment is the contractual promise that could be easily nullified if one of his wife's guests were to reveal the truth of Clare's identity. Their legally fraudulent (because of deceit, not because of rules against miscegenation which were not in New York statutes) marriage centers the novella's intrigue. The layers of promises that relate to racial intimacies compose the puzzle and the complexities of this story. At one point, as all of the truths of racial passing are about to be revealed, the husband who has, quite literally, been "playing in the dark" with respect to his wife's real race comes into a party to confront her. "The men had sprung forward. Felise had leapt between them. . . . She said quickly, 'Careful. You're the only white man here.' And the silver chill of her voice, as well as her words, were a warning" (ibid., 90). At this point the threat of his marriage's racial secret is literalized and physically dangerous.

Zora Hurston's *Their Eyes Were Watching God* explored Janie's evolution through three marriages, each one posing a different kind of threat to the freedom she yearned for. And in the novel's penultimate scene, a white judge and jury exonerate her of the murder of her last "husband" Tea Cake, allowing her to claim the independent selfhood she'd finally earned. Dana's freedom to marry a white man does her no good at all when she is snatched back to the era of slavery in Octavia Butler's *Kindred*, in fact, their relationship and the interracial permissibility that characterizes the sociality of their shared era is a potential threat to her survival in a past where enslavement and its customs are the norm and she is doubly vulnerable because her contemporary conduct violates those social norms. In Alice Walker's *The Color Purple*, Celie lives in constant terror with the man she married to escape the father who molested her. Similarly situated issues of identity, freedom, enslavement, and fugitivity weave throughout these novels of the black literary tradition and the right to and consequences of marriage and family. The promises that inhere seem a central thread that knots the arguable potential gained in the freedom by adhering to a promise that feels more like a threat, "You better not never tell nobody but God" (Walker 2006, 1).

There is an undeniable legal underbelly that links these narratives of the tradition, a facet that gives some reason for the constancy of marriage and the disarray of the family as an idée fixe in black literatures.

Although some might read this interest as sociology, the argument of this book is that the social is a consequential enactment of the legal. Just as contract rights extend from an implicit promise and are linked to the problematic histories of property, ontology renders evidentiary issues a complex terrain of race as visible, invisible, and perplexing "admixtures." None of these seem to resolve the legal questions that emerge as much as they constituted the necessity for additional legal fixes to the problematic and contradictory decisions that were rendered and became subsequently attached to racialized socialities. Black literature's investment in this conundrum comes with an imaginative intensity that derives its authoritative energy from the consistency of law's interpellations. It is not as if these literatures flaunt the legal parameters of its preoccupations with marriage, family, and the racialized vulnerabilities that inhere. But those relationships are nevertheless constitutive. Black authors who implicitly explore contract through the literary complexities of a promise do not so much illustrate a deliberate connectedness to the ways in which contract is a facet of black literature's boundedness to law. Instead their narrative interests discover this scaffolding as a *consequence* of the interest in the biosocial complexities of race. When race matters as legal history, contemporary reality, or as a facet of the imagination, the black literary project excavates this embedded textural relationship. One particularly compelling example that illustrates the potential for shared space between legal reasoning and literary imagination comes from Walter Mosley's 2004 novel, *The Man in My Basement*.

A Secluded Colored Neighborhood

Walter Mosley's protagonist Charles Blakey is propertied—he owns a large, "beautiful" home in Sag Harbor that has been in his family for seven generations; his race—"colored"—is evidence that has narrative importance; and he is offered a contract of fifty thousand dollars if he will rent his basement to a white man from Greenwich, Connecticut, who has a very particular set of conditions that have to be met if the two-month contract is to be signed and executed even though "we didn't take in white boarders in my part of the Sag Harbor. I was trying to understand why the real-estate agent . . . would even refer a white man to my neighborhood" (Mosley 2004, 5). Blakey is in need of the money because he has remortgaged the family home and that mortgage stands in arrears. Anniston Bennet is in need of the basement imprisonment he engages and endures—necessarily by a black man—because his guilt is racialized. With the characteristic determinative privilege of whiteness, a privilege that will allow him to self-determine his crime and his punishment, Bennet decides that a cell in a black man's basement will both contain and exculpate his guilt. It is not just any basement. Blakey's property is a strategic site—a space old and storied enough to contain the extraordinary confession that he extracts from his tenant, and even one that might shift the privileged arrangement that Bennet assumes is his to control. Although the contract is traditionally executed—Charles Blakey takes the money he offers (an offer and an acceptance form the basis of legal contract), the racialized narrative that began when the white man showed up in a colored neighborhood, reliably emerges as an accompaniment to the story's unfolding. Bennet produces a lock from an old slave ship to secure the door to the cell that Blakey finally agrees to build. "'It's an original lock used to hold down a line of slaves in the old slaving ships,' Bennet told me. 'It's over a hundred and fifty years old.' . . . I didn't feel the pang or tug of identity when slavery was mentioned. But that lock was a vicious thing" (ibid., 125).

Mosley's novel is Kafkaesque in its deeply signifying emplotment that unfolds in a language so moderate that the hauntingly wicked details of criminal guilt for which Bennet endures his sixty-day imprisonment seem incommensurate with the textual space they occupy. But the crime and punishment scenario structures the story enough so that the laws' facts consistently lie just within reach of the narrative. For example, the house that Blakey's family has owned for seven generations (an explicit narrative of property) comes from a history that was related to, but fugitive from legal enslavement: "The Blakeys were indentured servants who earned their freedom. . . . My parents were both very proud that their ancestors were never slaves" (17).

Blakey's home, of totally different lineage and standing than the Convent in Morrison's *Paradise* is still a threatened sanctuary. The mortgage contract that binds it is in arrears so its ownership is contested and threatened, and like the Convent, a white invasion unsettles the spirits of the place and makes the seclusion both have enjoyed no hiding place from the home's invasion. Mosley's novel actually embeds two properties—the decades-old family home as well as the jail Mosley constructs in the basement for the white entrepreneur whose crimes are nearly unspeakable. That second space transforms the place that was so proudly different from the homes of those neighborhood families, similarly secluded and similarly colored, who could not profess, as his family did, their distinction from families who had been enslaved. As a carceral space the basement becomes an environment that quite literally "holds" as many horrific secrets as the actual hold in Johnson's slave ship, as the incarcerated property once aboard the *Amistad* and the *Antelope*, and as the tourist boat in Paule Marshall's *Praisesong for the Widow* in which Avey Johnson is rocked back into the traumatic rememory of a middle passage voyage where she has the impression of "other bodies lying crowded in with her in the hot airless dark. Their suffering—the depth of it, the weight, and memory of it in the cramped space made hers of no consequence."[18] It is a quasi-legal holding space.

The fact that places shift their shapes along with people—that slavery as an indisputable past has a correlative and consequential lock on identity despite the regulation of laws and the progressive impulse of our societies—gives a story like *Paradise* as much potential as *Praisesong*. If we wander anywhere near a belief that seclusion from predatory public racism would be a panacea, we only need recall the alternative space of Ruby or the stories spilled in Blakey's basement.

The literary archive of contested and compromised black families matches the weight of often confounding legal claims like Jacqueline

Henley's classification in *Green v. the State of Louisiana* and the heft of the social reasoning that inflicts itself on judicial opinion like Bardwell's refusal. The consequence of centering identity in narrative locations — whether literary or legal — is the expressive moral knottiness of the situations that might emerge when legal or social solutions render a faux and vulnerable credibility. These fictions of identity feed the persistence of U.S. black literatures' visibilities. They are evident on Barnes and Noble bookshelves where African American literature, which seems to mean fiction written by black authors only, has shelves of its own, or the spate of recognition of black authors, scientists, public figures, artists, and others of historically noteworthy accomplishments during February's designated acknowledgment of a black American history.[19] Black literatures' interest in the black self as an object of inquiry models a national narrative that is regulated by an evolving but identity-centered legalized personhood alongside the slippery slope of the social.

Consider the way in which the Louisiana justice of the peace makes his claim to progressivism with a reference to bathrooms. Many who heard the news story found his "they use my bathroom" defense particularly droll. The contested bathroom site resurfaced in a 2010 book and its subsequent film, *The Help*, that helped one Durham, North Carolina, realtor understand why bathrooms were located in such odd places in the older homes she sold.[20] Katherine Stockett's book offered what was for some a riveting narrative about the domestic intimacy of whites and blacks in situations when black women worked for southern white families. The novel-like tenor of white panic regarding interracial contagion is evident in Stockett's imbalanced narrative focus on bathrooms. Although whites had no problem hiring blacks to perform duties that included the most intimate kinds of caretaking, back-breaking housekeeping, and challenging child-rearing in their homes, using the same bathroom as their "help" was seen as a step too far. Even though *The Help* was a fiction set in the 1960s, a similarly sourced disavowal from the justice regarding a fear of contagion in the twenty-first century illustrates how racial fictions still compete with facts. The narratives these legal fictions compose might engage a social promise or sometimes a legal contract—both of which turn on some shared interpretive domain of consideration and equity.

The fact is there cannot be *consensus ad idem* (meeting of the minds) when there is inequity that stands in the way of contractual equilibrium. That by itself makes the literary exposé a hybridity that nullifies or at least renders vulnerable any legally viable contractual potential, especially when the object of inquiry is some actualized version of a fully human black person. If slavery is always the historical location and literary precedent, even when enslavement itself is far removed from legal praxis, the very potential of a promise, or the constitution of a contract between persons who are black and white, or even between black persons, is always in a liminal state of questionable formation. This is why the narrative of Gloria Naylor's *Linden Hills* has such a twisted evolution. Everything recirculates to the control of an evil landowner Luther Nedeed who subjects his residents to contracts that return the land to him upon their deaths and that retain the authority to determine which level of the circle an approved black family might inhabit. Nedeed uses the contracts (the deeds) as a means of maintaining his ownership of the families who are hostage as much to their desire to live in Linden Hills as to his obligatory enforcement of its various clauses. They were always to be tenants, because Nedeed would contractually maintain ownership in perpetuity:

> They had the papers—actual deeds—that said this land was theirs as long as they sat on it, and sit they would. So now practically every black in Wayne County wanted to be a part of Linden Hills. . . . Only "certain" people got to live in Linden Hills . . . they kept sending in applications to the Tupelo Realty Corporation—and hoping. . . . Linden Hills—a place where people had worked hard, fought hard, and saved hard for the privilege to rest in the soft shadows of those heart-shaped trees. . . . They had a thousand years and a day to sit right there and forget what it meant to be black, because it meant working yourself to death just to stand still. (Naylor 1985, 16)

In fact, Nedeed's authority depended on his investment in a reliable inequity between their desire and his need. It was a contract. The ideological pivot of personhood, whether as something *in potentia* as in Bardwell's racist imaginings, or declared legally legible in the second trimester of *Roe v. Wade*, or as incoherent families in Walker's *The Color Purple*, demand some exemplary power of personhood. That personhood would ideally reside not in what they might be (as in evidence); or what they might possess (as in property); but in what acts they might execute that have legal legibility and authority—acts that are protected by the presumptive equity of contract. A secluded neighborhood might represent itself as a figurative sanctuary—just as Blakey's home of several generations offers, the convent in *Paradise* implies, and the residents of Linden Hills aspire toward. But each of these locations literally maintains itself through law. Despite that regulatory apparatus, the presumptive sanctuary of each is finally and violently breached: "They shoot the white girl first" (Morrison, *Paradise*, 1); Willa Nedeed bears the dead body of her son up from the basement stairs of her imprisonment in *Linden Hills*, and Anniston Bennet never emerges from Charles Blakey's basement.

However, as is true for evidentiary issues or the complex contestations of property, contracts are also vulnerable because black bodies are subject to an affective characterization that renders them suspect categories (actually a legal classification recognized in constitutional law) and that renders the rights they might claim contingent.

Liberal whiteness—a figural consequence of an imagined liberalism—centers its own properties as normative and worthy of protection. It renders as fugitive, if not imaginatively figurative, any project that might explore the consequences of an alternative stance with regard to a racialist-derived authoritarianism.

Mat Johnson's aggressively postmodern *Pym* is perhaps the best exemplar of the incredible landscape that still lies at the center of a racial imagination and that, in the way that Johnson's historicized pastiche accomplishes, follows the map of the (inevitably) terror-bound racism to a legacy of racialized panics. As in Doctorow's *Ragtime*, Johnson's *Pym* moves between fiction and factual histories that play with Edgar Allan Poe's earlier fictive scaffolding in a way that makes Poe's novel as well as Johnson's appear to be embedded stories discovered from a legitimate (real) document. As Jameson suggests, the postmodern engages "a new culture of the image or the simulacrum" making whatever it is that clarifies the distinction between real and imagined a reflexive blur, a constitutive dimension of imagined liberalism.[21] But even that perplexing provocation has a skeletal legal appeal. Mat Johnson's *Pym* makes literal that appeal in a cousin's collection of black memorabilia, which Booker claims as evidence: "'Why do you do it, then? Why do you collect all the slavery stuff?' . . . 'I'm collecting evidence' was what my cousin told me, and the great trial that Booker Jaynes was preparing for unfolded before me. In the captain's living quarters, office, and many storage lockers, crowded with artifacts as they were, the case was perpetually made, stuck in closing arguments with judgment ever forthcoming."[22] It's an evidentiary moment that reaches back to Johnson's *Middle Passage* where another ship's captain is similarly entailed with purloined property — treasure that could stand as evidence of the ship's fugitive trafficking, undermining his case that the human cargo in the ship's hold was any more a legitimate holding than these treasures stashed in his cabin: "Temple scrolls I found, precious tablets and works so exotic to my eyes that Falcon's crew of fortune hunters could have taken them only by midnight raids and murder" (Johnson 1998, 48). But which part of that cargo belonged to the captain, and which to the ship's owner as lawful chattel? What might be determined to be stolen property was an unsettling legal question, an eerie echo of those ones the courts took up with regard to the enslaved cargo who emerged from the ships' hold in the cases of the *Antelope* and *Amistad* and claimed their personhood.

There is good reason for these seafaring narratives to circumnavigate black fictions. The substance of the tradition is itself a complex diaspora of black Atlantic people and property, contracts formed on one continent and executed on another, evidence transported from one mooring place to another that, in the navigation, changed its legal shape if not its given name illustrating the fictive transubstantiation of how a person becomes a property. It's a rich terrain for a fiction. And whether the stories are located on the seas or drawn away from those ports into the dense landscapes that would populate the United States, the folk who traveled alongside, whether evidence or persons, waited for a legal space to state their names and testify to how their composition depended on the constitution of their bodies. In Williams's *Dessa Rose*, Dessa says, "I kept waiting for Nemi to read me." When the bodies were black the fictions were nearly determinative.

E. L. Doctorow was certainly not alone in discovering the hijack that a black character might exert. It was an element of narrative composition that white writers whose stories engaged the histories of U.S. slavery would discover. Some would find it a utility, others would surrender their narratives to the compositional consequence of dark matter. This was precisely what Toni Morrison explored in *Playing in the Dark* when she wrote: "Black slavery enriched the country's creative possibilities. . . . The result was a playground for the imagination. What rose up out of collective needs to allay internal fears and to rationalize external exploitation was an American Africanism — a fabricated brew of darkness, otherness, alarm and desire that is uniquely American" (Morrison 1993, 38).

The one element missing from Morrison's deeply resonant consideration is what it was that could reliably undergird the structural component of that "fabricated brew"; what *architecture* would render the Africanism Americanist — one that might engage its old continental history even as it set out its new continental cartographies? The playground does have an evident scaffold. Its foundations lie in the law, and this contingent legalism becomes a salient factor for the literature by whites who recognized the creative fiction of a person as property, or the kind of evidence that makes race matter, or the potential that might lie in a contractually enforceable promise from a person not fully free to execute that promise as an obligation. White writers would also discover in American Africanism a subject particularly compelling for a fictional imagination. But they would also find themselves hijacked by the black subject's consequential

legalisms. There is even evidence of a middle passage of legal confounded-
ness. In the last decade of the twentieth century, British writer Barry Unsworth recalled the constituent legalisms in two masterful works: *Sacred
Hunger* (1992) and its twenty-first-century sequel *The Quality of Mercy*
(2011). It's important, for this project on legal fictions in U.S. literatures,
to come full circle and to acknowledge the ways in which diasporic imaginations are subject to contingent racialized fictions.

When and Where "All the
Dark-Glass Boys" Enter

British novelist Barry Unsworth's *The Quality of Mercy* explores the rich conundrum where the factual histories of an event like the one on the *Antelope* makes the emergence of a literary fiction an almost necessary terrain in order to fully expose the legal absurdity. His novel engages the moment when experience, law, morality, and the imagination collide:

> "The slaves were cast into the sea in order to claim the insurance on them."
>
> "Lawful jettison," Kemp said. "There was a shortage of water— barely enough for the crew. Barton will testify to that also. I am fully entitled to the insurance money. . . ."
>
> "But the insurers are contesting the claim, as you know; they will say the jettisoning was not lawful, they will say there was water enough. . . . They will maintain that it is a crime under any circumstances to throw living persons over the deck of a ship on the only grounds that they are sick and like to die."
>
> "It is a contagion of madness." Kemp said. "We are talking about the ship's cargo. The negroes were acquired by lawful purchase on the Windward Coast of Africa. They were to have been sold at Kingston slave market in accordance with established practice. How can they be regarded as other than cargo? . . . It is madness. . . ."

"Entirely so, sir. . . . But the law has to deal with divergent interests. . . . The law has to stretch, sir."[1]

A British writer, Unsworth indicates the diaspora-wide influence of the text of slavery, and especially its origin in British common law that struggled to maintain, correct, and regulate the "madness" of legal slavery. A few pages past his novel's nod to Blackstone's *Commentaries*, where it acknowledges how slavery has necessitated an exponential growth of capital statutes that might deal with the rapidly evolving character(s) in law, *The Quality of Mercy* notes that "property is the thing sir, not the person"—the very threat that Charles Johnson's Rutherford faced aboard the *Republic* in *Middle Passage*. The compelling absurdity of this legalized ontology turns to fiction in order to navigate the figurative triangle. These are troubled waters to engage and white writers were as subject to these tides as those whose journeys I've illustrated in the chapters of this book.

The subsequently legally immutable characteristic of race was a subject too extraordinary for the nation's literature to miss. And the notion of contagion, implicit in Louisiana Judge Bardwell's argument of who might "even," in his regressive cosmopolitanism, use his personal toilet, is tied to the expressive social histories of the American South. It is evident as a particular theme in the mid-twentieth-century setting of Katherine Stockett's novel *The Help*.[2] Stockett's character Miss Hilly expresses the common concern: "'All these houses they're building without maid's quarters? It's just plain dangerous. Everybody knows they carry different kinds of diseases than we do'" (8). And later she explains that "nobody wants to sit down on a toilet seat they have to share with them" (185). Legalisms, including (tortious interference with) contract, imprisonment, and laws of property and custom, are critical to Stockett's very particularized imaginary of blacks and whites in the American South.

The seepage of biosocial excess threatened the new nation and found its ways into the cultural panics that attached to race. This was especially true with a new nation that would compose its own version of its British origins in Blackstone's legal *Commentaries* as well as inherit the judgments regarding social hierarchies. Unsworth's fiction exposes laws and practices as enduring a nearly desperate effort of statutory composition in order to keep up and regulate England's increasingly complex relationship to slavery. It was to evolve into a troubled legal history as well as an imaginative legal fiction that would trace the national evolution of persons, property, and evidence. *The Quality of Mercy* offers the argument of this problematic collusion:

> Can any man say at what point in this series of events and by what miraculous intervention, these black men and women ceased to be goods and reverted to humanity? Can we say that they were goods when lying chained below decks, goods while being cast overboard alive, yet not goods afterward when their chains were struck off? (Unsworth 2011, 192–193)

A Contagion of Madness

When Anna Julia Cooper wrote, in *A Voice from the South* that "when and where I enter . . . then and there the whole Negro race enters with me" she may have been more prescient than her contemporary W.E.B. Du Bois whose famed prediction about the twentieth century's color line has arguably earned wider renown.[3] But Cooper, writing in 1892—a decade earlier than Du Bois—was decidedly perceptive in her own notification regarding the haunt of a raced congregation of blacks effacing (or rendering invisible) any singular black presence. A collective racial inhabitation became so familiar that the idea of cognizable race was written into U.S. law as an immutable category. Ironically, even in federal notice, race is rarely understood in the vernacular as a synonym for whiteness. Instead, its unspoken and presumptively colored value is precisely the thing that the legal cognition of race maintains. The result of depending on the law to function and sustain a social regulation renders racial logic into a systematic practice with a pronounced legal and social utility. Its reach clearly exceeds its grasp, as literature by whites in the United States has illustrated throughout its national history whenever something about the narrative makes race matter.

Recall Harper Lee's *To Kill a Mockingbird*, the southern story of racial injustice that earned its attention because of the appealing characterization of the compassionate and just defense attorney Atticus Finch, who acted against the norms of his white community to satisfy the demands of justice. The essentially disappeared text of Lee's novel is the story about the town's black families, living on its periphery but providing the labor that sustains its economies and who are all effectively destroyed by a white girl's false claim of rape. However, neither the black victim's troubling circumstance nor his kin become the novel's remembered focus or its narrative destination. Instead, a spectacularly staged display of the bravery of white Atticus Finch in the face of his own white community's violent racisms and the accompanying compelling characterizations of his children, Scout and Jem, capture the reader's attention and memory.

In the same way that black Tom Robinson's death is an exemplary footnote to the social education of the white children rather than a narrative that substantively engages the text, the social drama and the legal determinism of the trial, Robinson's prison escape, his murder, and the retribution of the law frame a story for subaltern spectacle. Harper Lee writes that (much like an invisible man) Robinson "faded from the town's memory." Even as the children's society and their father's is suffused with racial actors and the differences race makes — the lesson of the novel is the juridical instantiation of whiteness as the normative value and instrumental standard. It is a practical law that binds the entire scenario of the trial and pinpoints the location of the legal fiction. Atticus Finch notes it as the lesson he wants his daughter to understand from the confusion of events that have been the focus of the town's white and black communities (even though the reader learns little to nothing of the substance of the black folk). There's something that critically regulates the confusion. He tells his daughter that it is: "In our courts, when it's a *white man's* word against a black man's, the *white man* always wins."[4] Once whiteness becomes the de facto regime of U.S. jurisprudence and the protected social value, the regulation of what will be the essence of quotidian displays and the literal and figural disembodiment of black folk seems as reasonable as it is necessary.

Certainly there is reason to question the novel's titular interest — this is about birds? — and to marvel that Atticus Finch's most memorable lesson to his children, indeed, the documented claim is that "it's a sin to kill a mockingbird."[5] It is a displacement that makes the lingering legal question — the death of an innocent black man who is shot by white law enforcement officers — a lawful evolution of everyday norms as structuring of the town's return to social order as perfectly ordinary and narratively related events. Robinson's futile attempt to escape the law has a destined and familiar consequence. His effort to conduct himself in a way other than the kind of narrative spectacle that his race signifies (he was, in fact, a deeply humane person who pitied the poorly used white girl) is already condemnatory. His transition from empathetic and helpful bystander to the accused, an indicted criminal, and a fugitive, and then, finally, a fugitive who is the victim of state ordered murder when he's shot by police, is read into the normative outcome of the trial. Ironically, despite the distinction of their moral character, Tom Robinson always had the same destination as Richard Wright's Bigger Thomas. Both are natural-born outlaws. Lee's Robinson discovers the way in which his fugitivity stands alongside the lawlessness of his predicament. Not to mention — literally not to mention — the tolerable sexual abuse of the Ewell daughter or the criminal family history that produces an addled Boo Radley as a plain statement about the value of lives lived in the shadow of well-to-do and fully enforceable whiteness that accompanies the strictly gendered and class-based tolerations of the town. The locative capture of this novel's story into a southern narrative told by a genteel and retiring southern white woman renegotiates the story's compositional risks. It is bound to a law of custom as well as legal procedure. Despite the danger that finally reaches Robinson, the objective portrayal of his body as the physical threat is a frank absurdity. But as long as Tom is alive he is (at least potentially) visible evidence. Even though his withered arm that means he could not have committed the crime he stands accused of, his body's deformity is factually invisible in the eyes of the law that that southern courtroom regulates. His body's blackness is on trial — not his character or the condition of his physical presence. His color renders the evidence of his incapacity socially invisible and legally moot.

The idea of evidentiary value is of paramount value in U.S. literatures that allow color to stand in for character. So the parallel stabilization of legal fora that also makes color matter gives a particular context to the event or occasion of the legal in American literatures. Being outside of the law, or a fugitive to its regulations is as dependable an outcome when race matters to Faulkner as it is a passing but nonetheless notable characteristic in Fitzgerald. It is the substantive national recognition that there is a certain composition of persons that matters. When E. L. Doctorow published *Ragtime* in 1975, his triad of families — one white, one Jewish, and one black — each has a particular challenge negotiating the changing terrain of politics and society in turn-of-the-century New Rochelle, New York. But it is the black family, loosely configured because there is no contractual bond that unites them, that engages the particular challenge of an identity-bound fugitivity.

In *Ragtime*, Coalhouse Walker — a black man — demands restitution from a group of firemen who maliciously destroy his automobile. They refuse and he seeks legal redress. The colored lawyer he consults refuses to represent his claim against Westchester firemen, ridiculing its priority as well as Walker's naïve interest in what the lawyer sees as a less than urgent claim for equal justice. When it becomes clear to Coalhouse that it is his color that stands in the way of equal treatment, he accepts the futility of his procedural claims and the fact that he is indeed left out (side of) the law. He acts accordingly, and in a series of dramatic events, he's shot to death by policemen outside of the mansion belonging to financier J. P. Morgan that he had held as a negotiating tool. Fredric Jameson's reading of this novel as a notable "crisis in historicity" refers to a crisis that is enabled as much by its loosened ties to evident historical moorings as it is by its absolute suture to anticipated structures of legal entanglements that advance the story (Jameson, 30). The legally unmoored black family, already a fugitive from the protections of an orderly social contract like marriage much less the protections of the law, is subsequently danger-ously vulnerable to the colored politics of the judicial actors in the story— the district attorney especially. Doctorow exposes the D.A.'s dilemma: "I can't give in to the coon. Even to hang him. I can't afford it. It would fin-ish me. . . . the D.A. giving in to a nigger? No, sir! It can't be done!" (Doc-torow, 242).

The law imposes a virtual reach, across to diaspora literatures like Barry Unsworth's, and inside of the textured composition of U.S. literatures. Residing outside of the law or having even the potential of a disparate negotiation of one's personhood within it becomes a racial touchstone. In William Faulkner's *Requiem for a Nun*, the court begs for black nanny Nancy's acquiescence to the regulatory impress of law. Nancy has mur-dered Temple Drake's infant and her response to the courtroom ritual that will determine her punishment is to utter an alternative regulation— a religious one, as her guide. One might reasonably recall the mother in James Baldwin's *Go Tell It on the Mountain* and her fear that there are only two choices in the world—jails and churches—in understanding both the charge that Nancy faces and her response:

> All you can say when they ask you to answer to a murder charge is Not Guilty. Otherwise, they can't even have a trial; they would have to hurry out and find another murderer before they could take the next official step. So they asked her, all correct and formal among the judges and lawyers and bailiffs and jury . . . nobody really listening since there was only one thing she could say. Except that she didn't say it: just raising her head enough to be heard plain—not loud: just plain—and said 'Guilty, Lord'—like that, disrupting and confounding and dispers-ing and flinging back two thousand years the whole edifice of corpus juris and rules of evidence we have been working to make stand up by itself ever since Caesar.[6]

Nancy's outlaw conduct is readable into a tradition that black writers easily recognized. Faulkner, intimately understanding the vexed locations of history and conduct for his southern stories, could not help but find a similarly unruly black subject and then subject her to a ritual that might regulate her conduct.

Notably, when F. Scott Fitzgerald needed a neutral legally cognizable testimonial in *The Great Gatsby*, he gave that role to a "colored" person.[7] Implicitly acknowledging that person's potential liabilities would adhere to prevalent stereotypes, Fitzgerald endowed his witness with characteristics that would grant him the authority his color might mitigate against. He renders the man nearly immune to stereotype and racial boundaries. Since the principal Fitzgerald characters are white, the appearance of a Negro in Gatsby is strategic. The plot calls for someone unquestionably outside of his narrative patterns. By using a man of color, something that satisfies the visible neutrality necessary for this witness, he also has to imbue the character with traits that would give him a credibility that his color ordinarily contradicts. So, in a very simple yet clearly intended characterization, Fitzgerald accomplishes all his needs by the designation of his race, and then a designation of the kind of colored man he was. Fitzgerald wrote: "A pale, well-dressed negro stepped near."[8] This unnamed colored man was different enough from the elegant and careless set of whites; all are suspect in the cover up of the accident. The Negro could not possibly be mistaken as a potential participant of the upper crust whites whose protocols of membership were already being breached by Nick Carraway. But he still needs reliability for the testimony he offers to the policeman: "It was a yellow car,' he [the Negro] said, a 'big yellow car. New.'" The policeman concedes this witness's potential credibility when he orders him to: "Come here and let's have your name" (139).

Fitzgerald's seemingly benign descriptive modifiers actually amplify the legal potential of this witness. At this moment in the narrative, the story needs a neutral person to report on the bad acts of the main characters. Although he is just a brief interlocutor, he is deftly drawn. Daisy, who was driving Gatsby's automobile, has killed Myrtle Wilson. It is a pivotal indication of the carelessness of the wealthy and a critical moment in the narrative. Only someone who stands fully and absolutely outside of this clubby bunch, whose membership or potential association with them, or even desire for an affiliation would be fully incredible, could stand as a viable witness for, or against them. Although arguably *de minimus* with regard to the rest of the text, Fitzgerald's selection, description, and the necessary architecture of this moment where the law becomes involved with the main characters is absolutely consistent with the utility of race as a legal fiction. On the other hand, with Faulkner, Nancy's racial guilt is presumptive, familiar, and socially cognizable. Faulkner captures the legal disparities inherent in racial location, even within the law, when he writes about the novel's jailed Negroes, who stare from behind prison cell bars. He compares them to white prisoners, asserting that the colored prisoners have none of the "tapping, the fidgeting or even holding, gripping the bars like white hands would be" (155). Unlike Faulkner's black folks, white prisoners are desperately unable to relinquish their bodies to the confines of the jail. But his shackled blacks seem to have no more body than synecdochic remnants, displaced property, that "all the owners of them need to look out with—to look out at the outdoors—the funerals, the passing, the people, the freedom, the sunlight, the free air . . . just the hands: not the eyes: just the hands lying there among the bars and looking out . . . just lying there among the interstices, not just at rest, but even restful, already shaped and easy and unanguished . . . the steel bars fitted them too without alarm or anguish" (Faulkner, 155–156).

Faulkner and Fitzgerald illustrate the ways in which the critical tracery of racialized legal fictions has been fully embedded in our national literature. They manage black bodies in ways that echo Harper Lee's classic novel, Mark Twain's *Puddn'head Wilson*, and even Flannery O'Connor's short story, "Everything that Rises Must Converge."[9]

O'Connor's story was written nearly four score years after Twain's exploration of a version of justice mediated through southern custom—which would mean the story turns on the ways in which race matters. Twain wrote about two infants who shared enough visible features that the black woman who is the mother of one of them (and who is light enough to pass for white) finds it not unreasonable at all to exchange the two babies, hoping for a better outcome for her biological child than his race would ordinarily dictate. The outcome of Twain's novel depends on a courtroom trial where the legal questions of identity and lineage are resolved. Despite the fact that the boys looked white, Twain's fiction explains the plotted reasonability of racial difference. It is the taint of one child's blackness—although not facially evident—that was embedded in his spirit and that gives sufficient explanation for his criminal conduct. He is discovered through the irrefutable evidence brought forward in a trial that allows the white child (now fully grown) to be restored to his place in society. Roxie's white appearing black son Tom (Chambers) is sold down the river. Twain's narrative depends on a relationship between evidence and race. His nouveau evidence—the science of fingerprinting—is first used to solve a puzzle that turns out to reveal not only the truth of the matter, but the fiction of race that the story has engaged. The lesson is one similar to the Rhinelander case. The law exists—or is utilized—in part to make certain that race is at least legally discoverable.

The law is similarly important, although not at first as apparent a thesis, in the O'Connor story where mothers and sons meet on a city bus. Their meeting is a visual illustration of the contractual principle of *consensus ad idem*. The identical hat that both women wear is a visible indicator that they now share (at least presumptively) a similar economic potential. O'Connor's use of these women's ostentatiously hatted heads to make this principle visible is a lovely example of fiction's allure. But the text of the story reveals the white woman quite literally cannot bear the fact that she has come to occupy the same economic space as a black woman. Meeting a Negro who had become, at least by socioeconomic class, her social doppelganger leads to a fatal stroke.

The story's brief reference to the gradual dismantling of de jure and de facto segregation anticipates the Civil Rights Act of 1964. That legislation's consequence, the integration of public facilities, becomes the force majeure of the story. Although it appears only briefly and even obliquely,

O'Connor's fleeting reference to the integrated buses allows the reader to understand the emotional ground of the story and how the era, the plan, and the potential focus of the fiction extends from that now violated public space. That reference to law holds the key to the character's pitiful devolution as she is forced to lower her social standing and ride an integrated bus. She dies as a result of the traumatic racial confrontation that was the consequence of legal change.

The Negro grandmother and son are merely local color in this story, the aggravating circumstance that forces Julian's mother's stroke—even its medical reality—the blood clotted in her brain and blocked her arterial flow. It is an evocative scene that recalls Alice Walker's phrase some two decades later from *In Search of Our Mothers' Gardens* when she asks, "What did it mean for a black woman to be an artist in our grandmothers' day?"[10] One imagines an artist as someone who might adorn herself with an extraordinary chapeau for a bus trip with a recalcitrant grandson, a hat with "a purple velvet flap came down on one side of it and stood up on the other; the rest of it was green and looked like a cushion with the stuffing out" (4). Pages later, when she describes the black woman on the bus whose "large lower lip was like a warning sign" the description of her hat is a mirror image of the language O'Connor used when describing the white grandmother from the "purple velvet flap" to the "cushion with the stuffing out" (16). The shared hat is a display of the economies of equality. In an age when such adornment, and especially when artistic sentiment were restricted by color and class and challenged by laws that urged an erasure of these dependable social differences, it could well have been a decision "cruel enough to stop the blood."[11] O'Connor completed "Everything that Rises" just at the time when the civil rights movement was making a difference in customs and conduct so entrenched that they connected intimately to ideas of the body—cleanliness, disease, as well as racial purity and contemporary manifestations of the eugenics movement that continued policies of state sanctioned sterilizations with African American women and the kind of social nonsense that led white families that employed black domestic workers to build separate toilet facilities for them.

From the perspective of whites, the disturbing reality was the Negro's increasingly visible presence in what they once protected as "their" society, men they had rendered invisible were now dangerously visible. The Foucauldian irony, of course, is that a mirror was the tool that accompanied this particular play in the dark, and it reflected that dire potential back onto the woman who saw through the glass, darkly. This is not the utopic mirror that Foucault imagines as a virtual space that gives visibility to oneself, but it is heterotopic—a deviance of space (a bending) that extends from its normative fabrication.[12]

This is precisely the kind of altered location that could produce O'Connor's mid-century short fiction just as easily as it could create the twenty-first century fiction in which a former Boston mayor, a white man, adopts two black brothers while their sister and biological mother secretly spy on the new, legal family, throughout the boys' childhoods. In Ann Patchett's *Run*, the great irony of the story is that the black mother who has released her sons to adoption by the mayor is not the legal parent of the girl that eventually goes to live with her "brothers" and the white father who has legally adopted them.[13] In fact, it is the contract of adoption that confers on them the legal familial relationship readers believe to be theirs throughout the story because their shared blackness seems a reasonable enough mark of their kinship despite the fact that their relatedness is a narratively compelling legal fiction. Once the girl becomes a legal member of somebody's family—the Irish-American Doyle clan—the brown-skinned adopted daughter inherits a Virgin Mary statue that belonged to the mayor's deceased wife—an oblique allusion, perhaps, to the immaculate conception of the girl's familial claim. It is at least a slight reference to the ways in which religion and law find their way into the composition of a black subject. The statue in the Doyle family home was contested property that set the stage for the legal scaffolding of Patchett's very contemporary and very racially cognizant story. At its beginning: "Bernadette had been dead two weeks when her sisters showed up in Doyle's living room asking for the statue back. They had no legal claim to it . . . but the statue had been in their family for four generations, passing down a maternal line from mother to daughter, and it was their intention to hold with tradition. . . . The rule in the past had always been to give it to the girl who most resembled the statue" (1).

And at the novel's end, the newly adopted brown-skinned Kenya was told that Doyle, the man who is now her legal father "had written it down that the statue would go to her, just in case anything ever happened. . . .' 'Why give it to me?' She reached out and laid a finger on the gold of the halo. She had only owned it one minute and already she never wanted to let it go. 'Because you're the daughter is why,' he said. 'The statue always goes to the daughter." The opening caveat of "the girl who most resembled the statue" had vanished (295). Patchett's elegant novel is a good illustration of how property, contract law, and evidence continued to matter when the object was race. An author's experience with U.S. racialisms might give it particular contour or focus, but race will out, even when its contagion seems to some an inexplicable madness.

THE DETAILS IN LAW'S NARRATIVES and its literary fictions are compelling, rich, and persistent. One could easily compose a substantial concordance of property issues, evidentiary matters, and/or contracts made, broken, or implied in U.S. black literatures. Although this book does document some of this as an indication of the viability and intersections within such a project, *Legal Fictions* is certainly not the definitive record of these instances. It is, however, evidence of the "'novelization' or 'novelizing protocols' of a collective imaginary" that exists in tandem with legal rule.[14] My interest is located less in sussing out and recording each of those persistent and exemplary narratives than in what I consider a factually necessary assertion that these legal traces exist, matter, and instantiate the biosociality of a persistent racial legibility mapped within the intersectionalities of identitarian fictions of law. What is important is to notice the patterns of collision between race and legal boundedness illustrated in chapter 3's opening instance of the obscure, meager-minded, and racist (former) judge in Louisiana, who wielded his authority in the law as if it were his mandate to preserve and protect white privilege.

To this end, the black fictions referenced here that narrativize legal matters confirm the legally bound hypervisibility of race. Whether we see it or simply suspect it, a deeply entrenched biosociality lies within. Perhaps the law's investment in racial legibility is a social necessity attached to the persistence of socioeconomic stratifications. These investments inevitably redound to literature's susceptibility to instantiations of the social as well as to its subsequent legal contestations.

This book's notice of the critical and persistent intersectionality of objectified racialisms does not convey a judgment regarding the desirability of this notice, but it is certainly a clarification for those who would imagine that race(d) literatures ended along with the era of de facto or de jure segregations. Reading critical legalisms into U.S. literary histories imagines these outcomes quite differently.[15] In law, judicial notice rules on and then facilitates the entry of admissible evidence in order for it to become part of the record. It is the work product of the legal procedure. Perhaps a literary imagination might be understood as the work product of the contract between law and society. As a fiction it can take advantage of imagination's free-floating fantasies while retaining just enough identificatory biosocialities to recall the legal origins.

The proffer of a promise that already has race as a substantive factor in the mediation of that promise, or the character of a person whose legal being has a history in law and whose body bears evidence of that history, renders the law deferential to its social histories and leaves the literary cognizant that its narrative may already be entailed by racial text. Racial reasoning is not much different from understanding the density of a cultural studies that would inject legal systems as a dimension of, rather than a dimension separable, from culture. Histories and their seemingly discrete predilections toward neatly confined periodizations are, as Jameson argues in *Postmodernism*, a "conception which allows for the presence and coexistence of a range of very different, yet subordinate features."[16]

Neither histories nor their periodizations can escape the muddle of cultures.

A narrative space is scaffolded and liminal. It lingers between the legal and literary, perhaps like precedent, and certainly suggestive of Morrison's idea of rememory. In this imaginative potential site narratives exchange interests. Things like obligation and moral commitment play, for just a moment, with the alternatives of composition and their "novel-like tenor." Contract, like the idea of property and the performance of evidence, is the luminous site where stories meet, shed a bit of their particularities, and move toward some structural utility. They are a "merging fluidity of forms," and black literatures acknowledge the composition of an inevitably quasi-legal meeting place. Although the site may have passed on, some memory of race lingers. Where and when the simulacrum is constituted, where signified meets signifier and one becomes the glass, and the other the thing seen, this play eventually finds its dark matter in the same manner that Ellison reminded his readers in *Invisible Man*: "I walked, struck by the merging fluidity of forms seen through the lenses. Could this be the way the world appeared to Rinehart? All the dark-glass boys? 'For now we see as through a glass darkly but then—but then—' I couldn't remember the rest" (491).

When legal ties seem to bind in black literatures—they inevitably experience the kind of incoherence that slavery's fractured legacy left its inheritors. But those stories, rescued, retold, recovered, and reassembled, make U.S. black literatures occupy a complex, nationally necessary, and precious terrain. Blacks entered the nation's fictions in the same way that we entered the nation—fully encumbered by a legal boundedness, an insistence on the fecundity of the jurisgenerative principle and the nation's experience of race. For the twentieth century especially, the civil rights activism that eventually centered *Brown v. Board of Education* as a defining text of the era, led legally accomplished rights to underscore the ways in which "constitutional experience . . . more than the logic of any theory [became] the validating force in law."[17] Black literatures remember, or at least reconstitute Ellison's "rest of the text" in their recompositions of our national narrative. Here all the dark-glass bodies find familiar locutions — precedents, promises, and penumbras — all constitutionally extant as long as U.S. legalisms and the composition of U.S. fictions regulate the quotidian narratives of our similarly everyday lives.

Preface

1 See Ellison's "The World and the Jug" in *Shadow and* Act, 140. Ellison's list of authors argues for the premise of my *BookMarks: Reading in Black and White*—that, given the opportunity to list a literary ancestry, black authors place themselves into relationships with elite writers of the traditional Western canon.

2 Among the most well known is John Callahan's masterwork, *In the African-American Grain*. My own *Moorings and Metaphors* would appropriately be included in those theoretical works that reached toward West Africa in a search for U.S. black fictions' memories of kin.

3 Notice that the posting of this certificate on an official site of the White House (WhiteHouse.gov) indicates the way the issue has been not only politicized but made an official communication of the Obama White House. See http://www.whitehouse.gov/blog/2011/04/27/president-oba mas-long-form-birth-certificate.

Introduction. Bound by Law

1 The NIH notes that data collection on race and/or ethnicity, required for clinical research that the NIH will support, is understood as "social-political constructs and should not be interpreted as being anthropological

in nature." See http://www.grants.nih.gov/grants/guidelines/notice-files/not-od-01–053.html.

2 David Walker's *Appeal to the Colored Citizens of the World* was self-published as an abolitionist tract in 1829 in Boston, and Sojourner Truth's *A'int I A Woman?* was delivered in 1851 at the Woman's Convention in Akron, Ohio.

3 Morrison. *Playing in the Dark: Whiteness and the Literary Imagination*. Morrison's effort is, at its most fundamental, a cartographic project. Her goals were to "draw a map, so to speak, of a critical geography and use that map to open as much space for discovery, intellectual adventure, and close exploration as did the original charting of the New World—without the mandate for conquest" (3). Once the lines of this map are drawn, the ways in which the demarcations maintain their sites are, in my judgment, a consequence of the law.

4 Here I am particularly drawn to Fred Moten's association of fugitivity to glossolalia as a surplus that I read as having an essential textural/textual potential. See Moten, *In the Break*, 35.

5 Ellison, *Invisible Man*. Recall the Invisible Man's opening encounter with the white man whom he assaults because the white man refuses to see him. It's an early introduction to the novel's dependence on an insistent and threatening existentialism that is consistently articulated through legal or quasi-legal scenarios. This opening event is a criminal assault, punishable under local and federal statutes.

6 *State v. Mann* (1829). In reading this case it becomes evident that the law may also be used as a means of distancing oneself from the legal resolution. The judge's protestations here that there was a "struggle" in his "own breast between the feelings of the man and the duty of the magistrate" is an oft-cited section, used to indicate that there may have been a humane repugnance to the social requisites of the slave state. A critical response might understand the text as consistent with Christian confession and forgiveness, which tolerated slavery and allows an endless cycle of repetition of the act and an always available redemption without a change in the system that benefited the men who wrote these decisions.

7 Orlando Patterson's perspective differs. In *Slavery and Social Death* he argues that the legal denial of a slave's personhood "is a fiction found only

in Western societies . . . that there has never existed a slave holding society, ancient or modern, that did not recognize a slave as a person in the
law" (22). Patterson's argument seems an effort to reconcile the conduct
and consequence of slavery, the relationships persons had with real lives.
This desirable situation is, however, belied by laws that actually bemoaned
the inability to act toward the enslaved as real persons, as *State v. Mann*
quite apparently declares. Certainly the law is perversely contradictory on
this matter, but the grant of citizenship was a grant that was inclusive of
the rights held by constitutional persons. In my judgment, the legal question effectively ends with those amendments. For a perceptive rereading
of Patterson's claim and insight that better addresses the legal question, see
Colin Dayan, *The Law Is a White Dog.* I find Dayan's decision in that book
to "follow the call of blood" a more compelling articulation of this complexity of law and act (Dayan, 43).

8 Foucault, *The History of Sexuality,* 137.

9 The discussion in the afterword to professors' Byrd and Gates's new edition of Toomer's *Cane* explains the contradictions of his legal status. In the
review, Lee writes: "Toomer's official record stands in marked, and sometimes confusing contrast. Registering for the draft in 1917 he was identified
as a Negro, as he was in a 1942 draft registration document. But in 1920 and
1930 federal census reports identified him as white. In 1931, when he married a white woman, both bride and groom were identified as white on the
marriage license" (Lee, "Scholars say Chronicler of Black Life Passed for
White").

10 The quoted text is the final line from Countee Cullen's Harlem Renaissance sonnet "Yet Do I Marvel." The complete couplet reads: "Yet do I
marvel at this curious thing / To make a poet black, and bid him sing!"

11 Berlant, *Anatomy of National Fantasy,* 1. Berlant's interest in understanding
how national identities formulate themselves, specifically within what she
calls "official" culture, is a way of viewing a project like this one, without
the disciplinary boundaries I impose here (see Berlant, 20).

12 Morrison, *Beloved. Beloved* could easily become the singular touchstone for
this project, as thoroughly bound to the legal as the novel becomes, and
as clearly tied to an imagined liberalism of idea and consequence. But the

point of this project is to indicate the breadth of this legal reach, so although Morrison's novels clearly are implicated, those used as illustrations of the legal constitution of black fictions exhibit the wide range of my thesis.

13 Baldwin, *Go Tell It on the Mountain.* The closed binary of this mother's imagination for her sons effectively becomes her own prison house, as well as her children's.

14 Shange, *For Colored Girls Who Have Considered Suicide When the Rainbow Is Enuf*, 44. The very form of this "choreopoem" testifies to its effort towards fugitivity, in wanting to escape a traditional linguistic formulary. Nevertheless, the stories of the "colored girls" reads into the familiar disciplined scripts of literary/legal compositions.

15 Auden, "Law Like Love." I often read this poem as "literature like law" because the freedom and lack of constraint that Auden delegates to love is like literature's thick and complicated narratives.

16 See, for example, *Citizens United v. Federal Election Commission* (2010). In a 5–4 vote the U.S. Supreme Court determined that media, being composed of persons, functioned under the protections of the first amendment free speech guarantees despite the corporate formation of that speech.

17 Locke, *Second Treatise on Civil Government*, "Of the Ends of Political Society and Government." Locke's Second Treatise traces the social evolution of natural rights into the common laws of a civil state and underscores the people's originary investment and ownership of those rights.

18 Locke, *Second Treatise*, chapter 9.

19 Morrison, *Playing in the Dark*, 3.

20 See Davis, "The Private Law of Race and Sex."

Chapter 1. The Claims of Property

1 *Virginia Declaration of Rights* (1776).

2 Harris, "Whiteness as Property."

3 *Dred Scott v. Sandford* (1857). The Civil Rights amendments adopted at the end of the Civil War, made slavery illegal, granted citizenship to formerly enslaved persons, and detached voting rights from race.

4 The phrase "badges and incidents" is from the Thirteenth Amendment and

attached to jurisprudence that subsequently determines whether or not conduct is a discriminatory remnant of the slavery.

5 Virginia Slave Code (1705).

6 In *U.S. v. Bhagat Singh Thind* (1923), Thind argued he was Caucasian as a result of his being Aryan. The court referenced the statute that Thind used to verify his argument was based on a popular notion of whiteness rather than the quickly advancing scientific argument regarding the anthropology of the races.

7 See Randall Kennedy's *Interracial Intimacies* for an especially cogent analysis of the ways in which protecting the value of white sociality translated into legal reasoning when it came to judicial decisions that involved a determination of race. In *White By Law*, Ian Lopez lists a wide variety of variables that rendered the legal standard unpredictable, explaining that courts "had to establish by law whether, for example, a petitioner's race was to be measured by skin color, facial features, national origin, language, culture, ancestry, the speculations of scientists, popular opinion or some combination of these factors" (1999, 2).

8 William Blackstone, *Commentaries on the Laws of England* 2 (Facsimile, 1979).

9 *Trustees of Dartmouth College v. Woodward*, 17 U.S. 518 (1819), 636.

10 Johnson, *Middle Passage*.

11 "Badges and incidents of slavery" is the language within the Thirteenth Amendment that abolished slavery. It has stood since that moment, as precedential standard that the courts have used to determine whether bias has an origin in enslavement. Cases regarding housing and voting rights are particularly read within this language.

12 Ellison, *Invisible Man*, 33. The Invisible Man actually dreams this is the text of the letter he carries in the briefcase. In this way, the letter actually becomes him, attached as it is to the symbol of his imagined professional personhood.

13 This question reflects the critical text of Brandeis and Warren's seminal essay, "The Right to Privacy" published in the *Harvard Law Review* in 1896. I write in detail about their argument in *Private Bodies, Public Texts* and it is relevant here. The essence of that argument, that the authors understood

property was a right that existed outside of a person and was an incorporeal right but that privacy was an intimate aspect of identity" (*Private Bodies*, 28), is consistent with the representation of property that found a fugitive and operationally illegible nuance as the Constitution was amended to "correct" the philosophy of persons as property.

14 Jameson, *Postmodernism*, 3.

15 Reid-Pharr, *Conjugal Unions*, 21.

16 Nella Larsen, *Quicksand* and *Passing*, ed., Deborah McDowell, 238. See also Elizabeth Smith-Pryor's *Property Rites* for a thorough reading of the Rhinelander case and its implications for the national preoccupation with a proper and reliable determination regarding racial categorization.

17 Toni Morrison, *Paradise*.

18 Coleridge, *Biographia Literaria*. Perhaps this is an unexpected reference in this context. But Coleridge's engagement with mimesis, fancy, and imagination grapple with the compelling intersectionality of law and literature. His explanation of "fixities" is a version of orderliness easily akin to legal reasoning. And his understanding of imagination as a repetitive act that attempts to reproduce the original (divine) creation is a version, in my judgment, of both precedent and rememory. Coleridge's interest in constituting the conditions of poetic imagination lead him toward an instrumental notion of fancy, one that serves his interest in fixities and allows a poetic imagination to emerge. This is a helpful reminder that the great investment literary theory has with Foucault has a generative thread — arguably a legal one — that deepens its interest in mimesis.

19 Cullen, "Yet Do I Marvel." See Intro, nt. 10.

20 Brown, *Clotel; or, The President's Daughter*.

21 Jacobs, *Incidents in the Life of a Slave Girl*.

22 British common law finds its source in Roman law, and the idea of property as a facet of the law began with the Romans. Real estate and slaves acquired "dominium" — and in U.S. law real estate and slaves were horribly merged. The legal conception lingered. See Richard Pipes, *Property and Freedom*, especially chapter 1 for a thorough review of this problematic history. Pipes explains the *utendi* and *abutendi* doctrine, noting that "the best-known Roman law definition described dominium as 'the right to use

and consume one's thing as allowed by law' (*ius utendi et abutendi re sua quatenus iuris ration patitur*)" (11).

23 McKoy, *When Whites Riot*. McKoy challenges the media representation of "race riots" as a version of black activism when, in fact, white violence was the provocation and the consequence.

24 Johnson, *Autobiography of an Ex-Colored Man*, 65.

25 This is the core of my argument in *Private Bodies* — that the social privilege and protections of the idea of privacy and its practice is assumed by white, heterosexual males and is always contestable by gendered, sexual, or racial others.

26 Morrison, *Paradise*, 1.

27 Morrison, "Home," 9–11.

28 Ibid., 10–11.

29 Ibid., 9.

30 Butler, *Kindred*.

31 Best, *The Fugitive's Property*, 37.

32 Shange, *For Colored Girls* and Bambara, *The Salt Eaters*.

33 Dixon, *Vanishing Rooms*.

34 Dickerson, "A Property of Being in Paule Marshall's *Brown Girl, Brownstones.*"

35 Perry, *Stigmata*.

36 Article I, Section 8 Clause 4 of the Constitution of the United States of America was amended by Congress in 1790 (Act of March 26, 1790, ch. 3, 1 Stat. 103).

37 Lopez, *White By Law*, 43.

Chapter 2. Bodies as Evidence

1 *The Antelope*, 23 U.S. 66 (1825). Also see http://supreme.justia.com/cases/federal/us/23/66/case.html; and *U.S. v. Libellants and Claimants of the Schooner Amistad*, 40 U.S. (15 Pet.) 518 (1841).

2 The U.S. Revenue Cutter Service, established as an armed maritime law enforcement service in 1790, was an early iteration of the U.S. Coast Guard.

3 Kermit Hall et al., *The Oxford Companion to the Supreme Court of the United*

States, 41. In *The Antelope*, John Noonan explains in detail the ships' routes, name changes, and the legal arguments of the circuit and Supreme Court cases.

4 Alfred Brophy et al., *Integrating* Spaces, 7.

5 John Quincy Adams, *Amistad Argument*, 116, 117.

6 David Bradley, *The Chaneysville Incident*.

7 Kenneth Warren, *What Was African American Literature?*

8 Crais and Scully, *Sara Baartman*, 5.

9 Baucom, *Specters of the Atlantic*, 15.

10 Jones, *Corregidora* and Williams, *Dessa Rose*.

11 Mosley, *The Last Days of Ptolemy Gray*.

12 Petry, "The Witness." All in-text citations are to the Naylor edition.

13 In a 1994 event that gained worldwide attention, Susan Smith of South Carolina drove the car with her two children in the back seat into a lake and later claimed she and her children had been car hijacked by a black man and that she ran desperately after the car trying to stop him. The man was a fiction that depended on an available and credible narrative of potential criminal conduct attached to the visible, expectational evidence of race.

14 Naylor, *Linden Hills*.

15 Kenan, *A Visitation of Spirits*.

16 Kennedy, *Interracial Intimacies*.

17 Wright, *A Father's Law*.

18 I make this argument in *BookMarks* noting that "the traditions of books and reading in African America have had a peculiarly interesting history in which the very presence of one marks the potential of the other. . . . Once the assumption of literacy was no longer the sole mark of an 'exceptional Negro,' black authors found a way to signal their authority . . . an updated version of a claim to having mastered the best of the intellectual habits of an educated elite" (8, 9).

19 Wright, *Native Son*.

20 Walker, *The Color Purple*, 182.

21 Williams, *Dessa Rose*, 9. All in-text citations are to this edition.

22 Ellison, *Invisible Man*, x.

23 Krueger, *Reading for the Law*.

24 Davis, *Maker of Saints.*

25 Krueger, 116, 117.

26 Baldwin, *Evidence of Things Not Seen.*

27 Walker, *Meridian*, 8.

28 Hurston, *Their Eyes Were Watching God.*

29 McCall, *Them: A Novel.*

30 Coleridge, *Biographia*, 99. Coleridge was responding to ideas that emerged from his conversations with William Wordsworth, who had been his neighbor and as the prelude to his composition of "The Ancient Mariner." Coleridge took his task to be to write characters that were "supernatural, or at least romantic; yet so as to transfer from our inward nature a human interest and a semblance of truth sufficient to procure for these shadows of imagination that 'willing suspension of disbelief for the moment, which constitutes poetic faith.'" It is possible to read these reflections in chapter 9 of the *Biographia* as having some legal correspondence — if we read the "shadows of imagination" as having some equivalency to penumbral legal reasoning that becomes precedent.

31 Butler, *Fledgling*, 2007.

Chapter 3. Composing Contract

1 Bardwell quote in the epigraph comes from an AP story as reported in *The Huffington Post*. See http://www.huffingtonpost.com/2009/10/15/inter racial-couple-denied_n_322784.html (3/18/10). The actual "disallowing" took place five months earlier, in November 2009.

2 For a discussion that connects these various legal decisions to Lorraine Hansberry's dramatic interpretation in *A Raisin in the Sun*, see Blakely and Shepard (2006), esp. 102–110. Earl Dickerson represented Carl Hansberry before the U.S. Supreme Court in his claim arguing the unconstitutionality of restrictive covenants in *Hansberry v. Lee* (1940). The court's decision was based on the limits of class action suits and was a narrow victory because the constitutionality of the covenants was not settled with *Hansberry*. However, before a decade had passed, *Shelly v. Kraemer* (1948) did successfully reach the constitutional question.

3 R. D. McIlwaine III, attorney for the state of Virginia, argued the case for the state. Chief Justice Warren interrupted, asking if the state could make similar arguments regarding religion. Mr. McIlwaine expressed the opinion that the evidence would "be stronger" with interracial rather than interreligious marriage. Justice Warren expressed some measure of disbelief asking, "How can you say this?" The oral arguments may be heard at http://encyclopediavirginia.org/media_player?mets_filename=evr3856mets.xml.

4 The Supreme Court granted certiorari in *United States v. Windsor*, a DOMA (Defense of Marriage Act) case, as well as in the case challenging California's Proposition 8 *Hollingsworth v. Perry*. In *Windsor* the Second Circuit held that sexual orientation was like race and deserved a heightened scrutiny and that DOMA would not survive that review. The court's determination regarding *Perry* could have jeopardized any state laws that excluded same sex couples because there would be no compelling interest the state protected in banning gay marriage. The court has positioned itself to follow its holding in *Loving* that gave marriage equality to interracial couples. In June 2013, the court ruled to overturn DOMA and extend federal benefits to same-sex couples. The court declined to decide *Perry*, effectively allowing same-sex marriages in California. Because the court did not rule on *Perry*, however, same-sex marriages in other states were not affected and *Loving* was not precedential.

5 In critical ways, Bardwell's illogic gave personhood to the unborn in the same way that antiabortion statutes argue over the stage at which an embryo might gain the right of visible personhood. *Roe v. Wade*, in my judgment is a *scientifically* flawed decision because of this stipulation: what would be an inevitably shifting notion of fetal viability.

6 *Loving v. Virginia* 388 U.S. 1 (1967).

7 Nella Larsen, *Passing*.

8 Du Bois, quoted in Elizabeth Smith-Pryor.

9 *Green v. City of New Orleans* (La. Ct. App. 1956).

10 Ibid., 79, 80.

11 Ibid., 79. Ironically, the little girl was eventually removed from the Green's home and, by order of the Bureau of Welfare, sent to a Negro-only orphan-

age, despite the court ruling that she was legally white. Randall Kennedy opens his discussion in *Interracial Intimacies* with this case, supplementing the court record with substantive interviews with principals and professionals who were involved with or had knowledge of the case.

12 The book referred to by the state's attorney was Albert Gordon's *Intermarriage, Interfaith, Interracial, Interethnic* (1964). Shortly after the state's introduction of this research, the attorney for the Lovings quoted material from the same text that undermined the argument formulated by the state, noting "the segregation of any group . . . is unthinkable and even dangerous to the body politic."

13 *Green v. City of New Orleans*, 77.

14 Smith-Pryor, *Property Rites*. Angela Onwuachi-Willig has written perhaps the most rigorous legal review of the case in "A Beautiful Lie"; and in *Private Bodies*, I write in detail about the ethics of privacy with a focus on the exposure Alice Jones Rhinelander suffered in the courtroom.

15 Kennedy, *Interracial Intimacies*.

16 Clymer, *Family Money*, 11–12.

17 One could argue there was indeed precedent for this kind of visible display. It was exactly what happened when enslaved Africans were subjected to sale on auction blocks and in market squares during the era of U.S. slavery.

18 Marshall, *Praisesong for the Widow*, 209.

19 Ethel Morgan Smith's (1997) Op-Ed in *The Baltimore Sun*, "Come and Be Black for Me" poignantly captures the irony of this month.

20 Comment made by audience member at *The Regulator Bookstore* in Durham, North Carolina, during conversation of Katherine Stockett's *The Help*, moderated by Kate Bartlett and Karla Holloway. January 21, 2010.

21 Jameson, *Cultural Logic*, 6.

22 Johnson, *Pym*, 100–101.

Epilogue. When and Where "All the Dark-Glass Boys" Enter

1 Unsworth, *The Quality of Mercy*, 29.

2 Stockett, *The Help*.

3 Cooper, *A Voice from the South*, 31.

4 Lee, *To Kill a Mockingbird*, 364.

5 Ibid., 147.

6 Faulkner, *Requiem for a Nun*, 157–158.

7 Fitzgerald, *The Great Gatsby*.

8 Ibid., 139.

9 Twain, *Puddn'Head Wilson*; Flannery O'Connor, "Everything that Rises Must Converge."

10 Walker, *In Search of Our Mothers' Gardens*, 223.

11 Ibid.

12 See Foucault, "Of Other Spaces" In this essay, "heterotopia" is a space of otherness, with a physicality and metaphysicality that Morrison's site of "rememory" recalls.

13 Patchett, *Run*.

14 This particularly trenchant phrase is from Ian Baucom's *Specters*, 16.

15 I mean to suggest here that a cultural or literary studies perspective reads the law differently from a scholar who understands the discipline of legal reasonings from within, rather than as law as social desiderata. Kenneth Warren's reading of the end of African American literature may well be an example of desire.

16 Jameson, *Postmodernism*, 4.

17 Cover, *Narrative, Violence, and the Law*, 131.

Adams, John Quincy. 1841. *Amistad Argument*. Available at http://avalon.law
.yale.edu/19th_century/amistad_002.asp.

The Antelope. 1825. 23 U.S. 66.

Auden, W. H. 1941. "Law Like Love." *Another Time*. New York: Random House.

Baldwin, James. 1970 (1953). *Go Tell It on the Mountain*. New York: Dell.

———. 1995 (1985). *The Evidence of Things Not Seen*. New York: Holt.

Bambara, Toni Cade. 1980. *The Salt Eaters*. New York: Random House.

Baucom, Ian. 2005. *Specters of the Atlantic: Finance Capital, Slavery, and the Philosophy of History*. Durham, NC: Duke University Press.

Berlant, Lauren. 1991. *The Anatomy of National Fantasy: Hawthorne, Utopia, and Everyday Life*. Chicago: University of Chicago Press.

Best, Stephen. 2004. *The Fugitive's Property: Law and the Poetics of Possession*. Chicago: University of Chicago Press.

Blackstone, William. 1979 (1765–1769). *Commentaries on the Laws of England*. Vol. 2. Facsimile ed. Chicago: University of Chicago Press.

Blakely, Robert, and Marcus Shepard. 2006. *Earl B. Dickerson: A Voice for Freedom and Equality*. Chicago: Northwestern University Press.

Bradley, David. 1990. *The Chaneysville Incident*. New York: Harper Perennial.

Brewer, Holly. 2005. *By Birth or Consent: Children, Law, and the Anglo-American Revolution in Authority*. Chapel Hill: University of North Carolina Press.

Brophy, Alfred, Alberto Lopez, and Kali Murray. 2011. *Integrating Spaces: Property Law and Race*. New York: Aspen.

Brown, William Wells. *Clotel; or, The President's Daughter*. 2000 (1853). New York: Modern Library (Random House).

Butler, Octavia. 2004 (1989). *Kindred*. Boston: Beacon Press.

————. 2007. *Fledgling*. New York: Grand Central.

Callahan, John. 2001. *In the African American Grain: Call and Response in Twentieth Century Black Fiction*. Bloomington: University of Illinois Press.

Carter, Stephen. 2007. *New England White*. New York: Alfred A. Knopf.

Cary, Lorene. 1995. *The Price of a Child*. New York: Knopf.

Chesnutt, Charles. 2012 (1901).*The Marrow of Tradition*. Greensboro, NC: Empire Books.

Citizens United v. Federal Election Commission. 2010. 130 S. Ct. 876.

Clymer, Jeffory A. 2012. *Family Money: Property, Race, and Literature in the Nineteenth Century*. New York: Oxford.

Coleridge, Samuel Taylor. 2011 (1817). *Biographia Literaria*. CreateSpace.

Cooper, Anna Julia. 1990 (1892). *A Voice from the South*. New York: Oxford University Press.

Cover, Robert. 1982. The Origins of Judicial Activism in the Protection of Minorities." *Yale Law Journal* 91: 1287–1316.

Crais, Clifton, and Pamela Scully. 2010. *Sara Baartman and the Hottentot Venus: A Ghost Story and a Biography*. Princeton, NJ: Princeton University Press.

Cullen, Countee. 1925. "Yet Do I Marvel." *Color*. New York: Harper and Brothers.

Davis, Adrienne. 1999. "The Private Law of Race and Sex: An Antebellum Perspective." *Stanford Law Review* 2: 221–288.

Davis, Thulani. 1997. *A Maker of Saints*. New York: Penguin.

Dayan, Colin. 2011. *The Law Is a White Dog: How Legal Rituals Make and Unmake Persons*. Princeton, NJ: Princeton University Press.

Dickerson, Vanessa. 1991. "A Property of Being in Paule Marshall's *Brown Girl, Brownstones*." *Obsidian* 2: 1–13.

Dixon, Melvin. 1991. *Vanishing Rooms*. Berkeley, CA: Cleis Press.

Doctorow, E. L. 1975. *Ragtime: A Novel*. New York: Random House.

Dred Scott v. Sandford. 1857. 60 U.S. 393.

Ellison, Ralph. 1995a (1963). *Shadow and Act*. New York: Vintage.

————. 1995b (1952). *Invisible Man*. New York: Vintage.

Faulkner, William. 2012 (1951). *Requiem for a Nun*. New York: Vintage.

Fitzgerald, F. Scott. 2004 (1924). *The Great Gatsby*. New York: Scribner.

Foucault, Michel. 1978. *The History of Sexuality*. Robert Hurley, trans. New York: Pantheon Books.

———. 1986. "Of Other Spaces." *Diacritics*, Vol. 16. No. 1.

Gordon, Albert I. 1964. *Intermarriage, Interfaith, Interracial, Interethnic*. Boston: Beacon Press.

Green v. City of New Orleans. 1956. 88 So. 2d 76 (La. Ct. App.).

Hall, Kermit, James Ely, Joel Grossman. 2005. *The Oxford Companion to the Supreme Court of the United States*. Oxford University Press.

Hansberry v. Lee. 1940. 311 U.S. 32.

Harris, Cheryl. 1993. "Whiteness as Property." *Harvard Law Review* 106, no. 8: 1709–1795.

Hollingsworth v. Perry. Currently under review by U.S. Supreme Court.

Holloway, Karla. 1991. *Moorings and Metaphors: Figures of Culture and Gender in Black Women's Literature*. New Brunswick, NJ: Rutgers University Press.

———. 2006. *BookMarks: Reading in Black and White*. New Brunswick, NJ: Rutgers University Press.

———. 2011. *Private Bodies, Public Texts: Race, Gender, and a Cultural Bioethics*. Durham, NC: Duke University Press.

Hurston, Zora Neale. 1998 (1937). *Their Eyes Were Watching God*. New York: Harper Perennial.

Jacobs, Harriet. 2002 (1861). *Incidents in the Life of a Slave Girl*. Mineola, NY: Dover Thrift Editions.

Jameson, Fredric. 1990. *Postmodernism; or the Cultural Logic of Late Capitalism*. Durham, NC: Duke University Press.

Johnson, Charles. 1998. *Middle Passage*. New York: Scribner's.

Johnson, Mat. 2011. *Pym*. New York: Random House.

Jones, Gayl. 1986. *Corregidora*. 1975. Boston: Beacon Press.

Kenan, Randall. 1987. *A Visitation of Spirits*. New York: Anchor Books.

Kennedy, Randall. 2004. *Interracial Intimacies: Marriage, Sex, Identity, and Adoption*. New York: Vintage.

Krueger, Christine. 2010. *Reading for the Law: British Literary History and Gender Advocacy*. Charlottesville: University of Virginia Press.

Larsen, Nella. 2004 (1929). *Passing*. New York: Dover.

———. 2011 (1928). *Quicksand*. Connecticut: Martino.

Lee, Felicia. 2010. "Scholars Say Chronicler of Black Life Passed for White." *New York Times*, December 26, 2010, C1.

Lee, Harper. 2010 (1960). *To Kill a Mockingbird*. New York: Harper.

Locke, John. 1690. "Of the Ends of Political Society and Government." *Second Treatise on Civil Government*. Available at http://www.constitution.org /jl/2ndtr19.htm.

Lopez, Ian F. Haney. 1996. *White by Law: The Legal Construction of Race*. New York: New York University Press.

Loving v. Virginia. 1967. 388 U.S. 1. Oral arguments may be heard at http:// encyclopediavirginia.org/media_player?mets_filename=evr3856metsxml.

Marshall, Paule. 1984. *Praisesong for the Widow*. New York: Plume.

———. 1996. *Browngirl, Brownstones*. New York: Feminist Press at CUNY.

McCall, Nathan. 2008. *Them: A Novel*. New York: Washington Square Press.

Morgan Smith, Ethel. 1997. "Come and Be Black for Me." *The Baltimore Sun*. Available at http://articles.baltimoresun.com/1997-02-26/news/1997057 094_1_black-kids-white-woman-african-american.

Morrison, Toni. 1973. *Sula*. New York: Alfred A. Knopf.

———. 1987. *Beloved*. New York: Alfred A. Knopf.

———. 1993. *Playing in the Dark: Whiteness and the Literary Imagination*. New York: Vintage.

———. 1997. "Home." *The House that Race Built: Black Americans, U.S. Terrain*. Edited by Wahneema Lubiano. Durham, NC: Duke University Press.

———. 1998. *Paradise*. New York: Alfred A. Knopf.

Mosley, Walter. 2004. *The Man in My Basement*. Boston: Back Bay Books.

———. 2010. *The Last Days of Ptolemy Gray*. New York: Riverhead Books.

Moten, Fred. 2003. *In the Break: The Aesthetics of Black Radical Tradition*. Minneapolis: University of Minnesota Press.

Naylor, Gloria. 1985. *Linden Hills*. New York: Ticknor and Fields.

Noonan, John. 1977. *The Antelope: The Ordeal of the Recaptured Africans in the Administrations of James Monroe and John Quincy Adams*. Berkeley: University of California Press.

O'Connor, Flannery. 1965. *Everything that Rises Must Converge*. New York: Farrar, Strauss, and Giroux.

Patchett, Ann. 2008. *Run*. New York: Harper Perennial.

Patterson, Orlando. 1985. *Slavery and Social Death: A Comparative Study*. Cambridge: Harvard University Press.

Perry, Phyllis Alesia. 1999. *Stigmata*. New York: Anchor Press.

Petry, Ann. 1995 (1971). "The Witness." In *Children of the Night: The Best Short Stories by Black Writers 1967 to the Present*. Edited by Gloria Naylor. New York: Little, Brown.

Pipes, Richard. 2000. *Property and Freedom*. New York: Vintage.

Reid-Pharr, Robert. 1999. *Conjugal Union: The Body, the House, and the Black American*. New York: Oxford University Press.

Shange, Ntozake. 1980. *For Colored Girls Who Have Considered Suicide When the Rainbow Is Enuf*. New York: Bantam Books.

Shelley v. Kraemer. 1948. 334 U.S. 1.

Smith-McKoy. 2001. *When Whites Riot: Writing Race and Violence in American and South African Cultures*. Madison, WI: University of Wisconsin Press.

Smith-Pryor, Elizabeth. 2009. *The Rhinelander Trial, Passing, and the Protection of Whiteness*. Chapel Hill: University of North Carolina Press.

State v. Mann. 1829. 13 N.C. (2 Dev.) 263.

Stockett, Katherine. 2009. *The Help*. New York: Putnam.

Toomer, Jean. 2011 (1923). *Cane*. Afterwords by Rudolph Byrd and Henry Louis Gates. New York: Norton.

Trustees of Dartmouth College v. Woodward. 1819. 17 U.S. 518: 636.

Twain, Mark. 1894. *The Tragedy of Pudd'nhead Wilson*. New York: Dover.

Unsworth, Barry. 1992. *Sacred Hunger*. New York: W. W. Norton.

———. 2011. *The Quality of Mercy*. New York: Nan A. Talese, Knopf Doubleday.

U.S. v. Bhagat Singh Thind. 1923. 261 U.S. 204.

U.S. v. Libellants and Claimants of the Schooner Amistad. 1841. 40 U.S. (15 Pet.) 518.

U.S. v. Windsor. Currently under review by U.S. Supreme Court.

Virginia Declaration of Rights. 1776. Available at http://www.nationalcenter.org/VirginiaDeclaration.html.

Virginia Slave Code. 1705. Available at http://www.law.du.edu/russell/lh/alh.docs.virginiaslaverystatutes.html.

Walker, Alice. 1990 (1976). *Meridian*. New York: Pocket Books.

———. 2003. *In Search of Our Mothers' Gardens*. New York: Mariner Books.

———. 2006 (1982). *The Color Purple*. New York: Mariner Books.

Warren, Kenneth. 2011. *What Was African American Literature?* Cambridge, MA: Harvard University Press.

Williams, Sherley Anne. 2010 (1986). *Dessa Rose*. New York: Harper Perennial.

Wright, Richard. 2005 (1940). *Native Son*. New York: Harper Perennial.

———. 2008. *A Father's Law*. New York: Harper Perennial.

ACKNOWLEDGMENTS

Thank you all. You offered generous sites for sanctuary, words that were wanted, gentle urges, quiet nudges, and certain spirits. You have assured that I have had a life in letters — stitched leaf-to-leaf. All of which I would have wanted, had I only known.

Chesnutt, Charles, *The Marrow of Tradition*, 37–39

child and children: fetal viability and, 107, 136n5; interracial adoptions and, 93–96, 122–23, 136n11, 137n12; of interracial marriages, 26, 90–92, 119–20, 136n5. *See also* family

Christianity, and property claims, 24–25, 42–43, 128n6. *See also* religion

citizenship: Constitution and, xiii, *xiv*, 1–3, 8, 15, 127n3; interracial marriages and, 99–100; legal cases and, 24, 130n3; personhood intersection with, xv, 2–3, 27–30, 31, 52–53, 133n36; presidency and, xiii, *xiv*, 1–3, 127n3; property claims and, 27–30, 31, 52–53, 133n36; race and, 127n3; visibility/invisibility of blacks and, xiii, 3; whites and, 53, 94

Citizens United v. Federal Election Commission (2010), 130n16

civil rights: interracial marriages in context of, 89, 92, 98–101, 136n4; visibility/invisibility of blacks and, 21, 120–21

Civil Rights Act of 1964, x–xi, *xi*, 120

Clymer, Jeffory, 97

Coleridge, Samuel Taylor, 36, 66–67, 86–87, 132n18, 135n30

color line, 1, 60, 92–93, 97, 113

Constitution (United States Constitution). *See* United States Constitution (Constitution)

consumption, in context of property claims, 37, 132n22

contagion, and fear of whites, 89, 90, 105, 112, 121–22

contracts: overview of, 15, 20, 89–93; in American literature, 122–23; black bodies and, 100, 107–8; evidence intersection with, 68, 99–100; fugitivity and, 101; housing covenants and, 90, 102–7, 135n2; imaginative liberalism and, 107–8; interracial adoptions and, 93–96, 136n11, 137n12; personhood and, 107, 137n14; property claims intersection with, 27–35, 99–100, 131n9; race and, 122–23; white privilege and, 103; whites' fear of contagion by blacks and, 89, 90, 105, 112. *See also* interracial marriages; marriage and marriage contracts

Copper, Anna Julia, 113

Corrigan v. Buckley (1926), 90

Crais, Clifton, 63

Cullen, Countee, "Yet Do I Marvel," 36, 129n10

Davis, Thulani, *Maker of Saints*, 80

Dayan, Colin, 128n7

Declaration of Independence, 15, 23

Defense of Marriage Act (DOMA), 136n4

diaspora literatures, 108, 110, 112, 117. *See also* geography of identity

Dickerson, Earl, 135n2

Dickerson, Vanessa, 52

Dixon, Melvin, *Vanishing Rooms*, 51

Doctorow, E. L., *Ragtime*, 107–8, 109, 116–17

Douglass, Frederick, 53–54

Dred Scott v. Sandford (1857), 24, 130n3

Du Bois, W.E.B., 1, 92–93, 113

dying declarations, as evidence, 60–62

Ellison, Ralph, ix, 127n1. *See also Invisible Man* (Ellison)

embodiment of blacks: blackness and, 3; evidence and, 21, 56, 59–60, 65, 67–68, 72, 77, 80; hearsay and, 60, 65, 67–68; laws in U.S. and, 6; personhood as separate from, 8, 128n7; property claims and, 26; scholarship on, 3–4

enslavement narratives, 5, 8–9. *See also* neo-slave narratives; slaves and slavery; *and specific writers*

ethics of personhood: evidence and, 84; property claims and, 16, 25, 28, 50, 52

evidence: overview of, 15, 19–20, 21, 55–59; black bodies and, 55–56, 74–77, 79, 83–84, 87; British common laws and, 56, 60, 83; contracts intersection with, 68, 99–100; embodiment of blacks and, 21, 56, 59, 72, 77, 80; ethics of personhood and, 84; fact and fiction relationship and, 73–74, 85–87, 135n30;

fugitivity and, 79–80, 86; imaginative liberalism and, 81–85; interracial adoptions and, 95, 136n11; marriage contracts intersection with, 75; neo-slave narratives, 65, 67–68, 87; property claims intersection with, 19–21, 56–59, 65, 77, 84–85, 87, 108, 111–13, 133nn1–3; public/private dichotomy and, 81–83; race and, 63, 65–66, 68–77, 84, 87–88, 115–20, 122–23, 134n13, 134n18; testimonials and, 75, 79, 82–84, 86; of things not seen, 72, 79, 81, 85–86; visibility/invisibility of blacks as, 72, 79–80, 102. *See also* hearsay (secondhand information)

fact and fiction relationship, and evidence, 63–67, 73–74, 85–87, 135n30

family: interracial marriages and, 91, 97–99, 104–5; marriages and, 101–2, 107. *See also* child and children

Faulkner, William, *Requiem for a Nun*, 116, 117–19

fetal viability, and law in U.S., 107, 136n5

Fitzgerald, F. Scott, *The Great Gatsby*, 116, 118–19

Foucault, Michel, 8, 20, 122, 132n18, 138n12

Fourteenth Amendment, x, 15

freedom, in context of marriage, 30–31, 100, 101

Fugitive Slave Act of 1850, 11, 32, 37

fugitivity: in American literature, 22, 116–17; in black fiction, 5, 10–11, 13–14, 128n4, 130n14; bodies as property and, 27; contracts and, 101; evidence and, 79–80, 86; legal precedent and, 14; property claims and, 27, 29, 44, 53–54; race and, 10, 22, 115–17

Gates, Henry Louis, 9–10, 129n9
geography of identity, 4–6, 20, 27, 109, 128n3. *See also* diaspora literatures
Gordon, Albert, 95, 136n11
Great Britain, 20, 81, 111–13. *See also* British common laws; *and specific writers*
Green v. City of New Orleans (1956), 89–96, 104–5, 107, 136n5, 136n11

Hansberry, Lorraine, *A Raisin in the Sun*, 90
Hansberry v. Lee (1940), 90, 135n2
Harris, Cheryl, 23–24, 32–33, 41, 91, 96
hearsay (secondhand information), 67; black bodies and, 63, 66; dying declarations and, 60–62; embodiment of blacks and, 60, 65, 67–68; enslavement narratives and, 60–64; fact and fiction relationship and, 63–67; imaginative liberalism and, 67; race and, 63, 68–71, 134n13; rape and, 67, 68–70; rememories and, 60–61, 64, 67–68,

71; testimonials and, 61–62, 64. *See also* evidence
heterotopia, 20, 122, 138n12
Hollingsworth v. Perry (under review), 136n4
Holloway, Karla: *BookMarks*, 3–4, 74–75, 127n1, 134n18; *Moorings and Metaphors*, 127n2; *Private Bodies, Public Texts*, 3, 99, 131n13, 133n25, 137n14
homes and housing covenants: contracts and, 90, 102–7, 135n2; religion intersection with, 42–43; sanctuary in, 19, 42–43, 46–49, 67, 104, 107; white privilege and, 103
Hurston, Zora Neale, *Their Eyes Were Watching God*, 78, 82–83, 84, 101

imagination, in context of race, 20, 107, 111
imaginative liberalism: overview of, 129n12; contracts and, 107–8; evidence and, 67, 81–85; hearsay and, 67; jails or churches closed binary and, 11–13, 64, 117, 130n13; property claims and, 35–41, 132n18
inheritance, and interracial marriages, 97–98
interracial adoptions, 93–96, 122–23, 136n11, 137n12
interracial marriages: in American literature, 119–120; biologized identity and, 99; black bodies and, 96, 98–99, 137n14, 137n17;

interracial marriages (*cont.*)
children of, 26, 90–92, 119–20;
citizenship and, 99–100; civil
rights and, 92; civil rights of
blacks and whites in context
of, 89, 92, 136n4; family and, 91,
97–99, 104–5; freedom in context
of, 101; inheritance and, 97–98;
property claims intersection with,
97–99; racial identity and, 20, 34,
60, 93, 95, 100–101, 137n12; white
privilege and, 93, 95–99, 137n14.
See also contracts; marriage and
marriage contracts
intersectionality, in black fiction,
21–22. *See also under* contracts;
evidence; property claims
invisibility/visibility, and things not
seen as evidence, 72, 79, 81, 85–86.
See also visibility/invisibility, in
context of white privilege; visi-
bility/invisibility of blacks
Invisible Man (Ellison): blackness
and, 5, 69, 125; evidence and, 19,
69–70, 79–81; fugitivity in, 85–86;
personhood and citizenship intersection in, 29, 39, 52, 131n12; postmodernism and, 5, 29; property
claims intersection with evidence
and, 85; racial identity as legal fiction and, 128n5; visibility/invisi-
bility of blacks in, 79–81; whites
and white privilege and, 81, 128n5.
See also Ellison, Ralph

Jacobs, Harriet, *Incidents in the Life of
a Slave Girl*, 36–37
jails or churches closed binary, 11–13,
64, 117, 130n13
Jameson, Fredric, 31, 108, 116–17, 124–
25
Jefferson, Thomas, 15, 36
Jim Crowism, 63, 65, 70–71, 82, 90
John, Marie-Elena, *Unburnable*, 8–9
Johnson, Charles. *See Middle Passage*
(Johnson)
Johnson, James Weldon, *Autobiog-
raphy of an Ex-Colored Man*, 39–
41
Johnson, Lyndon B., xi, *xi*
Johnson, Mat, *Pym*, 107–8
Jones, Alice (Rhinelander, Alice), 20,
34, 92, 96–100, 97–100, 120, 125,
137n14
Jones, Edward P., *The Known World*,
8–9
Jones, Gayl, *Corregidora*, 67, 100

Kenan, Randall, *A Visitation of
Spirits*, 72
Kennedy, Randall, 131n7, 136n11
King, Martin Luther, Jr., xi, *xi*
Krueger, Christine, 79–81, 83

Larsen, Nella: *Passing*, 20, 33–34, 92,
100; *Quicksand*, 33–34
laws in U.S.: biologized identity and,
2, 8, 9–10, 16, 129nn9–10; black
bodies and, xiii, 3, 16; blackness

and, 25; black writers as influenced by, x; British common laws
as source of, 14–17, 20, 130n17; citizenship and, x–xi, *xi, xiv,* 120; embodiment of blacks and, 6; ethical
personhood and, 16; intersectionality and, 21–22; Jim Crowism and,
63, 65, 70–71, 82, 90; legal precedent and, 13–15; neo-slave narratives and, 6–8, 128nn6–7; personhood history and, x–xiii, *xi, xii,* xv,
120; race and, xv; racial identity
as legal fiction and, 5–11, 21, 27,
128nn5–7, 129nn9–11; rememories
in context of precedent for, 6,
13–14; whiteness and, 25–26, 131n6.
See also United States Constitution (Constitution)
Lee, Felicia, 129n9
Lee, Harper, *To Kill a Mockingbird,*
114–16, 119
legal fiction, racial identity as construct of, 5–11, 21, 27, 128nn5–7,
129nn9–11. *See also* American literature and race; black writers
and fiction
legal precedent, 13–15
literature: diaspora, 108, 110, 112, 117;
as influence on black writers, ix,
127n1. *See also* American literature
and race; black writers and fiction;
and specific writers
Locke, John, 15–17, 130n17
Lopez, Ian, 53, 131n7

Loving v. Virginia (1967), 91–92, 95,
136n4, 137n12
Lydia (slave), 6–8, 21, 128nn6–7

Mann, John, 6–8, 21, 128nn6–7
marriage and marriage contracts:
overview of, 101–2; black bodies
and, 100–101; evidence intersection with, 75; family and, 101–2,
107; freedom in context of, 30–31,
100, 101; property claims and, 26,
30–31; racial identity as legal fiction and, 9–10, 129nn9–10; same
sex, 92, 136n4. *See also* contracts;
interracial marriages
Marshall, John, 27, 57–58
Marshall, Paule: *Brown Girl, Brownstones,* 51–52; *Praisesong for the
Widow,* 104
Mason, George, 23
McCall, Nathan. *Them,* 84–85
McIlwaine, R. D., III, 91, 136n3
McKoy, Sheila Smith, 38, 133n23
media, and representation of race
riots, 38, 133n23
Middle Passage (Johnson): contracts
intersection with property claims
in, 27–31, 34–35, 49–50; evidence
intersection with property claims
in, 56–59, 108; fugitive imagination
and, 29; marriage contract in context of civil rights in, 30–31, 100;
neo-slave narratives and, 8–9, 19;
personhood and citizenship inter-

Middle Passage (Johnson) (*cont.*)
section in, 27–30, 131n11; postmodernism and, 29, 31; property claims
in context of capitalism and,
27–31, 34–35, 49–50, 56–57, 87, 104,
108, 112; racial identity and, 28–32
Morgan Smith, Ethel, 137n19
Morris, Gouverneur, 23
Morrison, Toni: black bodies as evidence and, 76; black bodies as
property and, 32; ethics in context
of property claims and, 11; evidence and, 21, 76; fugitive imagination or fugitivity and, 11, 12,
109; geography of identity and,
4–5, 109, 128n3; "Home," 23, 46,
51; housing as sanctuary and, 19,
42–43, 46–49, 67, 104, 107; imaginative liberalism and, 11–13, 37,
129n12; interracial sexual relationships and, 93; legally visible/in-
visible and, 80; legal precedent in
black literature and, 13–14; neo-
slave narratives and, 8–9, 19; *Paradise*, 19, 34, 41–49, 51, 52, 76–77, 80,
104, 107; place versus personhood
and, 52; property claims and, 11,
19, 21, 31–32, 34, 51, 52; racial identity in context of property claims
and, 31–32, 34, 41–49; religious
and legal intersection and, 43; rememories and, 6, 13–14, 20, 61, 71,
138n12; *Sula*, 19, 21, 52, 93. *See also
Beloved* (Morrison)
Mosley, Walter: *Last Days of Ptolemy*

Gray, The, 68, 82; *Man in My Basement, The*, 20, 102–4
Moten, Fred, 128n4

Naylor, Gloria, *Linden Hills*, 19, 72,
75, 106–7
neo-slave narratives: overview of,
8–9; evidence and, 65, 67–68, 87;
laws in U.S. and, 6–8, 128nn6–7;
property claims and, 17, 19, 27, 41.
See also slaves and slavery; *specific
works*
nonhuman personhood, and Constitution, 15, 27, 130n16
Noonan, John, *The Antelope*, 133n3

Obama, Barack Hussein, xiii, *xiv*, 1–3,
127n3
O'Connor, Flannery, "Everything
that Rises Must Converge," 21, 119,
120–21
"one-drop" rule (biologized identity
and blood), 2, 8–10, 16, 26, 33, 99
origin narratives, and Constitution,
9, 18–19
outlaws/lawlessness: in American
literature, 115, 117–18; in black fiction, xiii, 3, 5, 27, 79

Patchett, Anne, *Run*, 122–23
Patterson, Orlando, 128n7
Perry, Phyllis Alesia, *Stigmata*, 52
Perry, Richard, *Montgomery's Chil-
dren*, 76–77
personhood: in American litera-

property claims (*cont.*)
89, 90, 105, 112, 121–22. *See also specific laws cases; specific writers*
public/private dichotomy, and evidence, 81–83

race and racial identity: overview
of, 1–3, 104–5, 127n1; biologized
identity and, 2, 8–10, 16, 26, 33, 99;
blackness and, 113; citizenship and,
127n3; color line and, 1, 60, 92–93,
97, 113; Constitution and, x, 2–3,
14; contracts and, 122–23; diaspora
literatures and, 108, 110, 112, 117;
evidence and, 63, 65–66, 68–77,
84, 87–88, 115–20, 122–23, 134n13,
134n18; fugitivity and, 10, 115–17;
geography of identity and, 4–6,
5–6, 20, 27, 109, 128n3; hearsay
and, 63, 68–71, 134n13; imagination in context of, 20, 107, 111;
interracial adoptions and, 93–96,
122–23, 136n11, 137n12; interracial
marriages and, 20, 34, 60, 93, 95,
100–101, 137n12; Jim Crowism
and, 63, 65, 70–71, 82, 90; laws in
U.S. and, xv; as legal fiction, 5–11,
21, 128nn5–7, 129nn9–11; marriage
and, 20, 26, 30–31, 34, 92, 96–100;
personhood and, 117–18; privilege and, 16; property claims and,
26, 28–34, 30–31, 33–34, 39, 41–49,
122–23; rape and, 63, 68–70;
slavery and, 30; testimonials and,

86; visibility/invisibility in context of white privilege and, 114–15,
120–22; visibility/invisibility of
blacks and, 25, 114–16, 120–22. *See
also* blacks and blackness; interracial marriages; race; whites and
whiteness
race riots, 37–39, 133n23
racial fictions. *See* American literature and race; black writers and
fiction
rape: evidence for, 63, 67, 68–70,
74; marriage as freedom from,
100; property claims and, 26, 38;
white's false claim of, 114, 115
Reid-Pharr, Robert, 32
religion: jails or churches closed
binary and, 11–13, 64, 117, 130n13;
property claims intersection with,
24–25, 42–43, 128n6
rememories: hearsay as evidence
and, 60–61, 64, 67–68, 71; heterotopia and, 20, 122, 138n12; legal
precedent and, 6, 13–14
Rhinelander, Alice (Alice Jones), 20,
34, 92, 96–100, 120, 125, 137n14
Rhinelander, Leonard (Kip), 20, 34,
92, 96–100, 125, 137n14
Rhinelander v. Rhinelander (1927), 20,
34, 92, 96–100, 125, 137n14
Roe v. Wade (1973), 107, 136n5
Roman laws, 8–9, 132n22
Rule of Naturalization or natural origin, x, xiii, 15, 53, 133n36

same sex marriages, 92, 136n4
sanctuary of homes, and property
claims, 19, 42–43, 46–49, 67, 131n11
Scully, Pamela, 63
secondhand information (hearsay).
  See hearsay (secondhand information)
sexual orientation, and marriage contract, 136n4
Shange, Ntozake, *For Colored
  Girls. . .* , 13, 50–51, 130n14
Shelley v. Kraemer (1948), 90, 135n2
slaves and slavery: black bodies
  and, 16; blackness and, 16; British
  slave trade and, 20, 112–13; in historic context, 24–26, 28, 32–33,
  131n4; marriage for black men
  versus, 30–31, 100; race and, 30;
  Thirteenth Amendment and, 24,
  131n4, 131n11; "unfree" whites versus, 32–33; visible/invisible black
  bodies and, 137n17. *See also* neo-
  slave narratives; *and specific cases,
  laws, and writers*
Smith, Susan, 71, 134n13
Smith-Pryor, Elizabeth, 96, 98–99
State v. Mann (1829), 6–8, 21,
  128nn6–7
Stockett, Katherine, *The Help*, 105, 112
Supreme Court, 6–8, 128nn6–7. *See
  also specific cases*

testimonials, as evidence, 61–62, 64,
  75, 79, 82–84, 86

things not seen, as evidence, 72, 79,
  81, 85–86
Thirteenth Amendment, 24, 131n4,
  131n11
Toomer, Jean, 9–10, 129nn9–10
*Trustees of Dartmouth College v.
  Woodward* (1857), 27, 131n9
Truth, Sojourner, 3, 128n3
Twain, Mark, *The Tragedy of Pudd'n-
  head Wilson*, 21, 119–20

"unfree" whites versus slaves, 32–33
United States Constitution (Constitution): bear witness right under,
  15; citizenship and, xiii, *xiv*, 1–3, 8,
  15, 127n3; contracts and, 15; nonhuman personhood and, 15, 27,
  130n16; origin narratives and, 9,
  18–19; personhood and, x, xii,
  2–3, 15–16; presidency in context
  of citizenship and, xiii, *xiv*, 1–3,
  127n3; property claims and, 15, 18;
  race and, x, 2–3, 14, 65–66; Rule of
  Naturalization or natural origin, x,
  xiii, 15, 53, 133n36; slavery in historic
  context and, 25, 28, 131n4; Thirteenth Amendment in, 24, 131n4,
  131n11; Fourteenth Amendment in,
  x, 15. *See also* contracts; evidence;
  laws in U.S.; property claims
United States Declaration of Independence, 15, 23
United States v. Bhagat Singh Thind
  (1923), 23, 131n6